Sunday School That Really Works

Sunday School That Really Works

A Strategy for Connecting Congregations and Communities

Steve R. Parr

Kregel
Academic & Professional

Sunday School That Really Works: A Strategy for Connecting Congregations and Communities

© 2010 Steve R. Parr

Published by Kregel Publications, a division of Kregel, Inc., P.O. Box 2607, Grand Rapids, MI 49501.

Library of Congress Cataloging-in-Publication Data
Parr, Steve R., 1958-
    A Sunday school that really works: a strategy for connecting congregations and communities / Steve R. Parr.
        p. cm.
    Includes bibliographical references.
    1. Sunday schools—Growth.   I. Title.
    BV1523.G75P37 2010
    268'.1—dc22
                                                        2009040748

ISBN 978-0-8254-3567-6

Printed in the United States of America
12 13 14 / 5 4

*To Carolyn, my wife and best friend,
for her unconditional love, support, and encouragement.
I thank the Lord for a godly wife and partner
in life and ministry.*

CONTENTS

FOREWORD

THE RUMORS OF ITS DEATH have been greatly exaggerated. Sunday school goes by many names in different churches. Still, most churchgoers recognize the more common name of this open small group that often meets on church campuses.

And not a small number of churchgoers think that the days of Sunday school's effectiveness as an evangelistic and assimilating arm of the church are passing quickly.

I should know. I was one of those Sunday school skeptics.

And then I tried something. I researched churches across America. My team looked at churches in denominations and at churches that had no affiliation with a denomination. We looked at small, medium, and large churches. We looked at churches in rural areas, suburban areas, urban areas, and transitioning areas. And I sent the research team forth with my bias that Sunday school was dying and losing its effectiveness. But I did my best to keep the study objective despite my bias.

You can probably anticipate the findings of the study. I was wrong. Dead wrong.

In some of the most effective evangelistic churches, Sunday school was the program of choice. In some of the best assimilating churches, Sunday school was the glue that held the people together. Ouch. It's tough to be that wrong.

But there is good news. The good news is that the old and sometimes maligned organization called Sunday school can still be an effective tool to move your church toward greater health. There is even more good news. You can have your own personal consultant to lead your church to becoming a healthier church. His name is Steve Parr. And he is the author of this gem of a book called *Sunday School That Really Works.*

I have known Dr. Parr for many years. I have known him as a leader in denominational work. I have known him as friend. I have known him as my doctoral student. And I have known him as one of the brightest minds alive today on Sunday school.

This book is just what many of our churches need. It may be what your church needs.

May I make a recommendation? Read this book. Then get some copies for key leaders in your church. Ask them to read this book. Then get additional copies for members throughout the church. I think they will be amazed. I know they will be motivated. And I would not be surprised if you see some really positive developments in your church.

Thank you, Steve Parr. You have made a great contribution to the health of the church. I recognized that reality the first time I read the book. But then I read the book a second time, something unusual for me. And I was even more encouraged.

This book is just that good.

Thom S. Rainer
President and CEO
LifeWay Christian Resources
Author of *Simple Life*

PREFACE

I HAVE HAD THE WONDERFUL privilege of being in hundreds of churches and sharing with thousands of Sunday school leaders. I love equipping and challenging key leaders so that they may in turn influence people to know Christ and to grow in their walk with Him. Thanks to so many of you who have graciously allowed me to share with you. This book is the result of my many years of experience, my passion to equip and touch lives, and your encouragement for me to write it down. It has been a longer journey then I anticipated, but I trust that God has guided everything including the timing.

I am grateful for the support of Dr. J. Robert White and the staff of the Georgia Baptist Convention. Dr. White encourages staff members to write and to grow to their fullest potential. I am a beneficiary of that philosophy, and I am indebted to the Georgia Baptist Convention for the role that the leaders and the staff have played in giving me the freedom and resources to pursue this project in addition to my ministry responsibilities.

I am grateful for many encouragers along the way as I have labored over this project. I want to express thanks to Dr. Thom Rainer, Dr. Ken Hemphill, Dr. Bobby Welch, Josh Hunt, Allan Taylor, Dr. Alvin Reid, and David Francis for your feedback and affirmation as I wrote this book. I am surrounded by an excellent staff who encourage me day in and day out: Dr. Tim Smith, Dr. Alan Folsom, Patrick Thompson, Randy Mullinax, Marc Merritt, Lucy Henry, Lynn Miller, and Sharon Nowak. I thank you for all that you do. Patrick Thompson was gracious in contributing the ideas for preschool, children, and student leaders in chapter 6. I am appreciative to my daughter, Lauren, for assisting with the first phase of editing, and my good friend,

Sandra Hamilton, for her assistance in the latter stages of editing and formatting in preparation for the publishers.

I am thankful for the excellent staff at Kregel Publications. They have been a blessing to me, and God is using the staff to touch many lives through publishing excellent Christian books and resources. You are a blessing to leaders like me who desire to maximize their influence for the cause of Christ.

I must express appreciation to my parents and my sister for the encouragement they have been to me throughout my life. They have always been supportive of me. They laid the foundation for the person who I am and who I am becoming as God does His work in my life.

Other than God Himself, my deepest gratitude belongs to my wife, Carolyn, for her unconditional love and support. My wife and my daughters, Leah, Lauren, and Larissa, have willingly sacrificed so that I might be on mission for the Father whether through traveling to equip leaders or to seclude myself to write as I am doing now. I love each of them with all of my heart.

Finally, I am thankful to God for His blessings and provision. It is only by His grace and power that I can accomplish anything at all. It is ultimately to His glory that I present this book and myself.

INTRODUCTION

It's Not "My Way or the Highway!"

I WANT TO BEGIN WITH a word to those of you who do not have a Sunday school and those who do have a Sunday school but call it by some other name. The word is *relax*. I am about to make a passionate argument on the merits of Sunday school. However, that does not make me an opponent of those who utilize small groups or reject the term *Sunday school*. My prayer for you is that you will be effective in reaching the unchurched, assimilating your new members, and discipling your members through the teaching and application of God's Word. I challenge you to use the strategy and the terms that enable you to accomplish those aims most effectively. I hope this book will provide insight that will help you be more effective as you follow the direction God is leading you. I confess that I am often frustrated by the rhetoric of those who speak against or decry what other churches are doing effectively.

In any case, I can point to churches that are effective in reaching the unchurched and discipling believers that have a fairly traditional Sunday school structure as well as those that are more innovative. I can also point to churches in each of those categories that are totally ineffective. I confess that I do have a bias, but it is not a bias that opposes the way other leaders fulfill the Great Commission.

I am going to use the word *Sunday school* descriptively throughout this book. It is a familiar term that I will use in this context to describe Bible study groups in local churches that are generally organized by age affinity (preschool, children, student, and adult) and ordinarily meet on Sunday morning immediately before or after the morning worship service. I acknowledge that the equivalent of a Sunday school class can meet at other times and be organized by various other affinities. As a matter of fact, most churches that have a Sunday school ministry would benefit from creating one or more groups that meet at a time other than Sunday morning in order to reach those who will never consider participating in one of the existing classes. I know of several churches that are currently leading what I call a "Sunday school plus" model with great effectiveness (Sunday school classes plus small groups during the week aimed at a different audience).

Perhaps you are considering whether you should dismantle your Sunday school and go to a small group model at a time other than Sunday morning. I hope that this book will assist you in that decision, and I pray that God would grant you wisdom and success. It is possible that you may need to reconsider Sunday school (though you may not choose to call it by that name) and move back to the strategy once you have a better understanding of its principles and original intent. I pray right now that God will speak to your heart as you read. My aim is not to convert you to anything but to challenge you and encourage you to develop a small group strategy that will enable your church to be more effective in evangelism and discipleship. Unlike other Sunday school books that you may have read in the past, the book you are about to read is not about ratios and numbers. It is filled with encouragement to provide leadership and influence attitudes. Therefore, I want you to relax, and I hope that you also enjoy considering what it is like to have a Sunday school that really works.

CHAPTER 1

Does Sunday School Still Work?

"IT DOESN'T WORK!" I HAVE heard this statement often in my ministry. A leader is doing all that he or she can, or at least all that he or she knows how to do, and yet the Sunday school is struggling. A Sunday school teacher works hard at preparing and delivering a lesson and wants the class to grow; however, no guests are ever present. I have had the privilege of leading Sunday schools to grow and helping others for more than twenty years. Sometimes a pastor or Sunday school teacher will speak with me following a presentation to explain why the tools I have just shared with him or her will not work. However, I can point to not only dozens but also hundreds of churches that have growing Sunday school ministries. Sometimes the growing Sunday school is in the same community as the person who has expressed to me that it does not work.

I once read an interesting metaphor describing church strategies. It noted that Dakota tribal wisdom says when you discover you are riding a dead horse, the best strategy is to dismount. However, churches often find themselves trying other strategies. Consider the following ten ways that churches and organizations deal with the problem of riding dead horses:

10. Provide additional funding to increase the dead horse's performance.
9. Provide training to teach people how to ride dead horses.
8. Appoint a committee to revive the dead horse.
7. Change the person riding the dead horse.
6. Say things like: "This is the way we always have ridden this horse."
5. Appoint a committee to study the dead horse.
4. Harness several dead horses together for increased speed.
3. Pass a resolution declaring: "The horse is not dead."
2. Arrange to visit other sites to see how they ride dead horses.
1. Buy a stronger whip.

Is the expectation of growing a Sunday school today the equivalent of riding a dead horse? If it does not work, then why is it working in so many churches? Dr. Thom Rainer, while leading a team of researchers for the Billy Graham School of Evangelism, conducted a study of North America's most effective evangelistic churches. The results revealed that a Sunday school strategy, or its equivalent by another name, was a common component of the churches' plan for reaching the community. He concluded: "If any program-based methodology proved to be a dynamic tool for these evangelistic churches, it was the Sunday school program. Most of the leaders of these churches were amused at the prophesies of the decline or death of Sunday school. When we asked them why such predictions were being made, they had a unified response: The problem with nonevangelistic Sunday schools is not the program itself; the problem is failure to use the program as an intentional evangelistic tool."[1]

---

1. Thom Rainer, *Effective Evangelistic Churches: Successful Churches Reveal What Works and What Doesn't* (Nashville: Broadman & Holman, 1996), 16.

WHAT IS A SUNDAY SCHOOL THAT WORKS?

An effective Sunday school strategy can have a dramatic effect on the evangelistic results of the church, and effective evangelism has the potential to impact the Sunday school in a positive way.

The Georgia Baptist Convention (GBC), a state convention of Southern Baptist churches, annually identifies its top one hundred fastest growing Sunday schools. The 2008 study revealed that those one hundred churches, which amounted to 2.8 percent of the GBC churches, accounted for 11 percent of the baptisms in the year of study (see table 1.1). The top twenty-five in each of the following categories are considered: Small—those averaging fewer than 100 in Sunday school attendance; Intermediate—those averaging 100 to 199 in attendance; Medium—those averaging 200 to 399 in attendance; and Large—those averaging more than 400 in attendance. As the figures demonstrate, these one hundred churches baptized 58 percent more than they did three years ago. By contrast, the other 3,469 churches in our state denomination had baptized 6.2 percent fewer than they had three years ago.

On the other side, effective evangelism can have a profound effect on the Sunday school. The annual reports submitted by our churches revealed that 23 percent provide training in personal evangelism for their members.[2] By contrast, a study of our state's fastest growing Sunday schools revealed that 85 percent provide personal evangelism training.[3] It is not hard to figure out that as more people are trained and challenged to share their faith, more people trust Christ as their Savior. As more people trust Christ, more people become involved in the Sunday school or the small groups of the church.

---

2. Steve Parr, *Georgia's Top Evangelistic Churches: Ten Lessons from the Most Effective Churches* (Atlanta: GBC Research, 2008), 8.
3. Steve Parr, "Georgia's Fastest Growing Sunday Schools: Ten Common Factors" (Atlanta: GBC Research, 2001), pdf available at gabaptist.org under Free Resources link.

Table 1.1. Baptism Increase of Georgia Baptist Convention (GBC) Churches with Fastest Growing Sunday Schools

	Number of baptisms in year		change (%)
	2005	2008	
25 fastest growing small Sunday schools	112	408	+264
25 fastest growing intermediate Sunday schools	226	620	+174
25 fastest growing medium Sunday schools	521	725	+ 39
25 fastest growing large Sunday schools	1,395	1,828	+ 31
Totals for the top 100 GBC churches with the fastest growing Sunday schools	2,254	3,581	+ 58
Other 3,469 GBC churches	30,002	28,133	-6.2
All GBC churches	32,256	31,714	-1.6

Source: Statistical information for Georgia Baptist Convention churches based on a comparison of Annual Church Profiles for 2005 and 2008, by Research Services of the Georgia Baptist Convention.
Note: The top twenty-five in each of the following categories are considered: Small— those averaging fewer than 100 in Sunday school attendance; Intermediate—those averaging 100 to 199 in attendance; Medium—those averaging 200 to 399 in attendance; and Large—those averaging more than 400 in attendance.

Further research has revealed that participation in Sunday school makes a dramatic difference in the assimilation of a new believer (see figure 1.1). The survey questioned people who had received Christ as Savior five years earlier. Of those who immediately became active in Sunday school, 83 percent were still active five years later. By contrast, only 16 percent were still active if they did not become active in Sunday school immediately after becoming a believer. What a dramatic difference! Commenting on these findings, the researchers concluded: "With this type of data, one might expect churches to give high priority to getting new members involved in a small group immediately. We certainly found the formerly unchurched to have an enthusiastic view of small groups, particularly Sunday school. . . . The picture is clear: the formerly unchurched 'stick to' a church when they get involved in a small group. Let us pray that more churches will learn this lesson."[4]

Figure 1.1. New Believer Assimilation Rate

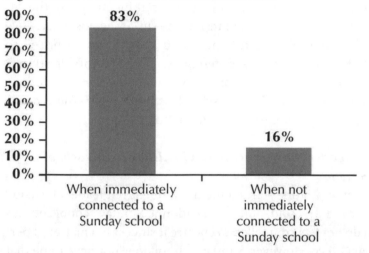

Source: Data from Thom S. Rainer, *Surprising Insights from the Unchurched and Proven Ways to Reach Them* (Grand Rapids: Zondervan, 2008), 118–20.

The principles that affect the growth of a Sunday school are not necessarily geographical. You can find churches in every region of North America that have growing Sunday school ministries. You can find them in rural, suburban, and urban areas. Following research that affirmed this perspective, Rainer quoted a pastor who, in his own pastorates, observed, "The bottom line is that basic Sunday school principles worked in a blue-collar Florida church, a California yuppie church, and a Bible-belt middle-class Texas church. Sunday school works if

---

4. Thom S. Rainer, *Surprising Insights from the Unchurched and Proven Ways to Reach Them* (Grand Rapids: Zondervan, 2008), 118–20.

it is worked right."[5] The principles also can be effective cross-denominationally. He goes on to say: "In our study of 576 effective evangelistic churches, we found the Sunday school to be one of the most important factors in the churches' success. Since all of these churches were Southern Baptist, I expected that the Sunday school factor was something unique to the denomination. . . . But when I tested the survey against nearly five hundred non–Southern Baptist churches, I was surprised to find little to no statistical differences, except in worship styles."[6]

Given this information, why then are many of today's leaders dismissing Sunday school as a strategy? The reasons that many have done so include the following:

Some leaders have never had a healthy Sunday school experience

Some pastors, staff members, and church leaders have experienced dry, cold, dull, and academic Sunday school settings and do not feel compelled to endure it since it is a matter of personal choice. However, Sunday school does not have to be that way, and it is not that way in all churches. Some leaders assume that it cannot work if they have not personally seen it happen in their setting. I jokingly say that the number one reason people do not want to go to Sunday school is because they *have* been. Some leaders have had the same experience and do not have any other context from which to draw their conclusions.

Some leaders have never been taught the principles of Sunday school growth

I recently asked a group of master of divinity graduates what they had learned about Sunday school growth in their

---

5. Rainer, *Effective Evangelistic Churches*, 97.
6. Thom S. Rainer, *High Expectations: The Remarkable Secret for Keeping People in Your Church* (Nashville: Broadman & Holman, 1999), 23–24.

seminary experience. Only one of about sixty students could point to any academic training in this area. Ordinarily, if the pastor does not have the tools and the knowledge, neither will the members. The result is that many pastors go into a church that has the basic Sunday school structure (rooms, classes, teachers, rolls, curriculum, etc.), but the Sunday school is life-less and cold. I am not aware of anyone with expertise who pro-poses that Sunday school can thrive on autopilot. Yet, many leaders draw the conclusion that it does not work because the basic structure is present and there are no results.

Some leaders assume Sunday school does not work because another prominent leader has dismissed it as ineffective

The other leader is often successful in preaching, growing the worship attendance, and/or perhaps reaching people for Christ. Surely, Sunday school cannot work if it does not work in his church! The success of the leader in other areas may lead those who hear him to conclude that Sunday school cannot be relevant if it did not work for him. In addition, many leaders dismiss it outright because it is not an innovative approach in their estimation. However, their innovation and success cannot be interpreted to mean that Sunday school cannot be effective because they did not choose to use it as a strategy or because it is not the latest trend. On the contrary, many churches have struggled because they have tried to emulate these innovative churches, perhaps because of their fascina-tion with the innovations and their desire to be on the cut-ting edge. I believe in being innovative. However, I am more concerned with being effective. Some church leaders have concluded that Sunday school cannot be effective today be-cause it is not a new innovation. It is not new in the context that it was developed in a previous generation. However, it is relatively new in the context of the history of Christianity (see figure 1.2). Robert Raikes started the first Sunday school about 220 years ago. Sunday school has been in existence as an education and evangelism tool only during the most recent 11 percent of Christian history. The real question is not whether it is new, old, contemporary, or out of date. The most important question is whether it can be effectively used to evangelize and to educate in the Christian church today and in the future.

Figure 1.2. Sunday School: New Tool or Old?

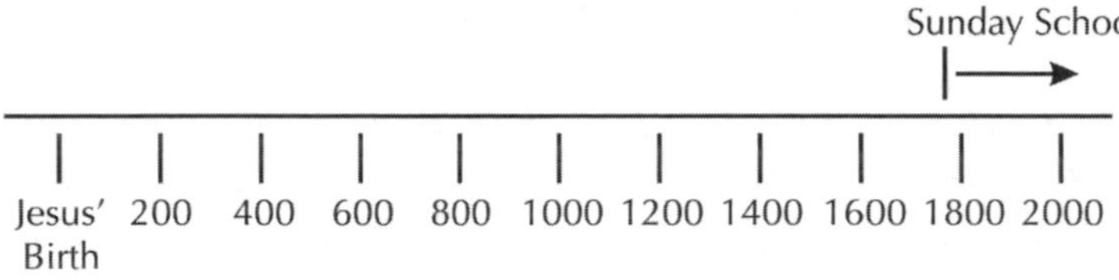

Sunday School

$\mapsto$

Jesus' 200 400 600 800 1000 1200 1400 1600 1800 2000
Birth

Years of Christian History

Some leaders are unwilling to pay the price to lead the Sunday school to be healthy and growing

I will state a simple fact here without any apology or hesitation: leading the Sunday school to be healthy and growing is hard work. It is a high-maintenance strategy involving a large number of the congregation. The results can also have a high return. Sunday school is a tool that can involve every generation in the church in evangelism, Bible study, fellowship, ministry, and assimilation of new members. Do you have a saw in your garage? Go out to your garage and watch it work. It will not work if it is not in someone's hand. It is only a tool. Take the saw and hold it. It still does not work, does it? You have to know what to do with it. You have to keep the blade sharp and use it in the way that it was designed. Sunday school is a tool. You cannot sit back and watch it work. You have to sharpen it and apply it in the way that it is intended. The problem is not that Sunday school will not work. The problem is that we have

22

good-hearted teachers and leaders who have not been taught how to use the tool.

How can you know if it is working correctly? A Sunday school that really works will see at least three results.

The lost will be reached. The word *lost* is not a contemporary term but a biblical term often used to describe the state of a person who does not have a personal relationship with Jesus Christ. A class or a church can express the purpose of the Sunday school in many ways. Ultimately, I believe the purpose is to enable the church to strategically embrace and engage the Great Commission as stated by Jesus in Matthew 28:18–20. A Sunday school that works is one that equips and challenges the classes or small groups to move beyond the church walls and into the community, working together to share the gospel and bring people to Christ. Sadly, many classes meet for Bible study and give no consideration, time, or effort to this end. The result is that many people have concluded that Sunday school does not work, when in reality the Sunday school has lost focus and moved off of the intended track.

Lives will be changed. God's Word is powerful, and people are transformed as they are exposed to it. The problem that many Sunday school classes encounter is not the power of God's Word but the anemic presentation of unprepared or passionless teachers. The teachers I am describing love God and love their church. However, they may not have been equipped and are often not motivated to prepare and present the lesson with effectiveness. It certainly cannot help their attitude if the pastor or other leaders are talking down the value of Sunday school. Additionally, many are unaware that they are ineffective. They have concluded that the purpose of Sunday school is to study the Bible, and that is what they are doing. Therefore, they see themselves as successful. James 1:22 says, "But be doers of the word, and not hearers only, deceiving yourselves." A Bible study in a Sunday school class or a small group of any kind is not intended to be an academic exercise. It is intended to be an encounter with God that affects the participants' lives day in and day out. An encounter with God's Word should lead to personal spiritual growth that in turn leads to life change. The teacher of the class bears the responsibility of confronting the class members with the truth of God's Word with the aim of personal application and the spiritual growth of all members.

Leaders will be sent. Rick Warren rightly states that the measure of a healthy church is not its seating capacity but its sending capacity.[7] The same is true of a Sunday school class. A consistent encounter with God through the study of His Word will lead many participants out of the class into ministry. Many children and students who grow up in a healthy Sunday school will heed God's call to missions and ministry. All members will feel compelled to find their place of service within the existing class or externally as God sends them. I know what many of you are thinking, and you are correct. Each class will have members who do not attend regularly as well as those who attend and choose to do nothing but sit and listen. The teacher of a healthy class will be frustrated by that fact but will understand that moving one, two, or three class members into leadership each year can make a huge impact in the life of the church.

SUNDAY SCHOOL: RELEVANT OR A RELIC?

A Sunday school strategy requires a tremendous amount of time and energy on the part of the pastor, staff, and church leaders. It is a waste of energy and resources if it is irrelevant. Some will argue that it is not relevant because of the failure of their church or the failure of others to do it successfully. They will conclude that it does not work, and therefore any church that utilizes the strategy is outdated. To draw this

---

7. Rick Warren, *The Purpose Driven Church* (Grand Rapids: Zondervan, 1995), 32.

conclusion dismisses the fact that many churches still have healthy and growing Sunday school ministries. Remember that others will dismiss Sunday school as irrelevant merely because the strategy is more than two hundred years old. Still others will suggest that it is irrelevant because some prominent churches have found success with other models. The assumption they make is that the new model must necessarily replace an older model for the church to move forward.

The conclusion that they will draw is based on improper criteria. What makes Sunday school relevant is its purpose wedded with appropriate practices. The purpose is to enable the church to strategically embrace and engage the Great Commission. That is accomplished when classes work together to take the gospel into their community (*Go therefore and make disciples of all the nations*), initiate new Christians into the community of believers (*baptizing them in the name of the Father and of the Son and the Holy Spirit*), and lead those believers to have a growing relationship with Jesus Christ (*teaching them to observe all things I have commanded you; and lo I am with you always, even to the end of the age*).[8] It is not appropriate to assign irrelevance to the strategy just because some have lost focus and have failed to appropriately and effectively utilize the Sunday school. The problem is that many Sunday school ministries, if not most, have lost focus. Those that have stayed focused on, or have refocused on, the biblical purpose can be referred to in many ways, but not as irrelevant.

Dr. Ken Hemphill is a tremendous leader, pastor, and church growth leader. He wrote a book entitled *Revitalizing the Sunday Morning Dinosaur*. He addresses the issue of relevance and provides practical tools for implementing a Sunday school strategy effectively. Hemphill has personally led churches with thriving Sunday schools and mentored thousands of pastors and leaders.

---

8. Matthew 28:19–20.

He states: "It is my conviction that the Sunday school has not lost its effectiveness as a growth tool, but that we no longer use it for its intended purpose."[9] How does Hemphill frame the purpose of Sunday school? He builds it upon the Great Commission. He points out that growth is not the aim of the Sunday school ministry: "*Obedience to the Great Commission, not church growth, is the appropriate goal for any church. Church growth results from obedience to the Great Commission.*"[10]

Gene Mims, author of *Kingdom Principles for Church Growth*, defines Sunday school in terms of the group's focus: "An open group is primarily an evangelistic Bible study group or event comprised of an intentional mix of both believers and unbelievers. The focus is evangelism, the context is Bible study, and the intent is to begin assimilation."[11] Sunday school will always be relevant so long as leaders apply the strategy with the focus Mims describes.

One of the leading authorities on church growth in Southern Baptist life is Dr. Thom Rainer. He currently serves as the President of LifeWay Christian Resources and formerly served as Dean of the Billy Graham School of Evangelism at The Southern Baptist Theological Seminary. He is the author of numerous books and builds most of his writing projects on thorough research of churches within and outside of Southern Baptist life. You will be hard pressed to read a book by Rainer that does not touch on the issue of Sunday school at some point. Following years of research on church health and growth, he continues to conclude that the Sunday school is relevant and can be effective.

Following his research of the most effective evangelistic

9. Ken Hemphill, *Revitalizing the Sunday Morning Dinosaur: A Sunday School Growth Strategy for the 21st Century* (Nashville: Broadman & Holman, 1996), 2.
10. Ibid., 35.
11. Gene Mims, *Kingdom Principles for Church Growth* (Nashville: Lifeway Christian Resources, 1994), 102.

churches in North America, he concluded: "Contrary to some critics, effective Sunday schools do not use archaic methods. No long-standing organization can survive two hundred years without methodological adaptation. The Sunday schools in many of these evangelistic churches today are vibrant organizations used effectively to teach and reach thousands."[12] He further concludes:

> Leaders have not been oblivious to comments about the prospective demise of the Sunday school. They expressed bewilderment that a methodology so effective in their churches was declared terminally ill by pundits. Indeed, several pastors shared that they had listened carefully to the critics, trying to determine if they and their churches were about to be left behind in a future methodological wave. But ultimately all came back to the position that Sunday school is neither ill nor dying nor dead. On the contrary, Sunday school *done well*, is one of the most God-blessed methodologies in the recent history of the church.[13]

Sunday school is relevant if it is done well and correctly focused. It is obviously not the only tool that is available to the church. However, it is a significant tool that a church can use to corporately engage the Great Commission. It involves all generations, preschool through senior adult, and involves a majority of the congregation. On an average Sunday, 70 percent of worship attendees in our state denomination attend a Sunday school class. That includes all churches. The healthier Sunday schools often have 80 to 90 percent of the worship attendees present. Sunday school is hardly irrelevant if 70 percent of the attendees are participating.

---

12. Rainer, *Effective Evangelistic Churches*, 82.
13. Ibid., 90.

Further, Sunday school classes tend to be organized by age groupings or life stages. Think of the advantages of this organizational structure. Prior to worship the high school students meet together, young adults meet together, senior adults meet together, and so on. Who is best at reaching high school students? College students? Young adults? Classes are organized to reach their affinity group. The same can be said for the assimilation of new members. A new member can be assigned to a group in a similar life stage. Who best helps a middle school student assimilate once he or she comes to know Christ? Obviously, it is other middle school students. If you do not believe me you should try assigning the next middle school boy who trusts Christ as Savior to the senior adult ladies class. Guess what? He will not be assimilated. An educational advantage certainly exists when we place children in a group where they can study God's Word on their intellectual and spiritual level. The same is true for all age groupings. In summary, a Sunday school done well enables the church to engage all components of the Great Commission within a single strategy (go, make disciples, baptize, teach). That is what makes Sunday school relevant.

SHOULD WE CALL IT SOMETHING OTHER THAN "SUNDAY SCHOOL"?

Behind the scenes: *I am getting downright discouraged. I faithfully prepare a lesson each week and do my very best to involve the class. I spend a lot of time and try not to be caught waiting until the last minute. Everyone seems to enjoy my teaching. I am not a professional, but people do respond and tell me that they are appreciative. A couple of members have even told me that I am the best teacher they have ever had. Our class really has a lot of depth and I know how to get into the "meat" of the Word. On one hand I am faithfully preparing and teaching the Bible, and on the other hand our class lacks any enthusiasm or motivation. I am most discouraged because we never have any guests. Occasionally someone will drop by, but it is the exception more than the rule. I don't remember the last time we had a guest who returned. People just don't seem to be interested in attending any more. I want to talk to the pastor about this. People do not want to go to "Sunday school" in today's culture. Those who already attend are in the habit, but new people are simply not going to respond. I believe if we called it something other than "Sunday school" we could attract more guests and turn our attendance around.*

Why is it called "Sunday school" in the first place? Do you know how Sunday school got started? It did not begin as a small group strategy. An Anglican layman named Robert Raikes started the first Sunday school around 1780. He lived in England during the time of the industrial revolution. His primary ministry was to prisoners at that time, and he observed that most of the men in prison were uneducated. As industry was expanding, many parents took advantage of the economic opportunities by sending their children to work in the factories, which excluded them from any formal education. Raikes set up and organized groups for children to go to school in the homes of their teachers on their day off to learn to read and for religious education. Thus, they went to *school* on *Sunday.*

What do you suppose they used for a reading text? Obviously, they did not have the types of resources that we are so accustomed to today. They learned to read using the Bible as their textbook. The children were learning to read, and the text began to have an effect on many lives. Raikes was well meaning in his desire to improve literacy, but the strategy was a divine design as children were exposed to the gospel and many trusted Christ as Savior. The strategy flourished with more than 250,000 children enrolled in Sunday school within the first four years, and the weekly attendance grew in various locations to 400,000 within thirty years.

Sunday schools began springing up in America by 1785

and spread rapidly over the next fifty years. Adult classes were incorporated into the strategy by the late 1800s. The strategy grew from its starting point of literacy and religious education for children to a strategy of small group Christian education (Bible study) and outreach for all ages.

Sunday school evolved as a cross-denominational strategy. Perhaps no denomination has adopted the term and the strategy with greater fervor than Southern Baptists. The strategy flourished for so many years because of the evangelistic component. While the international Sunday school movement shifted away from the priority of accomplishing evangelism and conversion through Sunday school work, Southern Baptists made a conscious decision to use Sunday school as the outreach arm of the church. The result was an evangelistic harvest from Sunday school that was unequaled by any other denomination.[14]

We might ask why do so many churches call the strategy "Sunday school," given that it is not a school and it does not exclusively meet on Sunday? The primary reason is familiarity. Sunday school is a familiar term and is understood to be a Bible study that meets on Sunday morning. Many churches have chosen to change the term because it is not descriptive or because of their conviction that it may hinder participation. You may be surprised to know that the name of the strategy is of little consequence to the unchurched. Following a study of formerly unchurched adults, the researchers concluded: "Interestingly, we did notice a slight transition from the no-menclature 'Sunday school.' Almost 20 percent of the churches in our study called their Sunday morning small group 'Bible study.' This shift was made because of the churches' perception of how the name 'Sunday school' is received. No formerly

---

14. Charles S. Kelley Jr., *How Did They Do It? The Story of Southern Baptist Evangelism* (Covington, LA: Insight Press, 1993), 98.

unchurched expressed concerns about the name."[15] The same principle applied to the name of the church.

David Francis, director of Sunday school for Lifeway Christian Resources, conducted a project around 400 Southern Baptist churches identified as "vibrant" to determine what kind of small group structure the churches operated. Gathering information from church Web sites and phone calls, he was able to gather information on 376 (94 percent) of the "vibrant" churches. Of those churches, 87.5 percent operated Sunday school or a functionally comparable on-campus program scheduled adjacent to the primary worship service. Small groups were operated by 12.5 percent, with the groups meeting primarily off campus at times other than Sunday morning. To describe the program, 53 percent of the vibrant churches used only the words "Sunday school" to describe the program; 26 percent used terms like Bible study, Bible fellowships, LIFE groups, or other terms; and 8 percent used Sunday school together with another term.[16]

A study of Georgia's one hundred fastest growing Sunday schools revealed that 79 percent used the term "Sunday school" compared with 82 percent of all Georgia Baptist Convention churches. The preponderance of use of the term "Sunday school" is influenced to some degree by geography and by denominational emphasis. You can find churches using the term that are thriving as well as those that are struggling. Likewise, you can find churches that call it by names already mentioned, such as Bible study or Bible fellowship, as well as other terms such as cell groups, small groups, life groups, community groups, life change groups, connection groups, or home groups. In fact, you will find thriving churches and struggling churches using any of these terms. I have observed

---

15. Rainer, *Surprising Insights from the Unchurched*, 47.
16. David Francis, "Simple Churches Have Intentional Sunday Schools," *Facts and Trends* (November/December 2006): 11, http://www.lifeway. com/lwc/files/lwcF_corp_factsandtrends_06NovDec.pdf.

many churches that have changed the title from Sunday school to one of the other terms thinking that new people would be attracted and attendance would increase. However, they failed to do something that was vastly more important. They failed to change the focus, and the name is not nearly as important as what you do with it. People attend because they are invited, they return because they have an enjoyable experience, and they attend regularly because they develop relationships.

Should it be called something other than Sunday school? What you call it is a minor issue. The advantage of using the term "Sunday school" is familiarity. The disadvantage is that it may evoke negative impressions in those who have had bad experiences in the past. The advantage of using another term is that you may get a slightly better response from students and young adults. The disadvantage is that some leaders will assume that the title is the issue rather than the principles and practices that make small groups work and will not make the adjustments that are really needed. Use your best judgment on the title. But most importantly, be sure to establish a Great Commission focus.

DISCUSSION QUESTIONS

1. How would you characterize the attitude of key leaders in your congregation toward Sunday school ministry? In what ways does this attitude affect its health?

2. How would you characterize the congregation's understanding of the purpose of the Sunday school? In what ways does that understanding affect the health and effectiveness of the Sunday school ministry?

3. How would you characterize your knowledge of the principles of Sunday school health and growth? What are some ways that your leaders can be equipped with the knowledge needed to lead the Sunday school effectively?

4. What do you call "Sunday school" in your church? What are some of the strengths and weaknesses of this designation? How can you compensate for the weaknesses?

CHAPTER 2

The Foundation for a Sunday School That Works

SUNDAY SCHOOL DID NOT EMERGE as a ministry of the church until the late 1700s. However, the principles that support a healthy Sunday school or small group strategy are rooted in the Scriptures. The Gospel of Luke provides a view of Jesus' leadership that is progressive, logical, and worthy of imitation.

THE SUNDAY SCHOOL EXPERIENCE OF JESUS

No, Jesus never attended or led a Sunday school class. Sunday school is not even mentioned in the Bible. However, Jesus is ultimately our model for living, leadership, and ministry. Did Jesus ever participate in or lead a small group? If so, where did the small group fit into His leadership strategy? What can we learn from His leadership that will enable us to develop and lead Sunday school classes that can have maximum impact? Let us consider four principles of personal growth and four principles of leadership from the Gospel of Luke that can help you effectively lead a Sunday school class.

Jesus' growth was socially, intellectually, physically, and spiritually balanced

And Jesus increased in wisdom and stature, and in favor with God and with people. (Luke 2:52 HCSB)

The Gospels are silent on the details of Jesus' life between the ages of twelve and thirty. Some facts can be gleaned through analysis of the Gospels. It is certain that He learned the trade of a carpenter and that His father, Joseph, died sometime during that span. The passage in Luke 2:52 is the concluding thought after the incident in which Jesus was left behind in Jerusalem and later found by His parents in the temple interacting with the religious scholars. Thus Luke provides his readers with a concluding summary of the years between this event and Jesus' baptism.[1]

The key lesson in this passage for the leader is the growth of Jesus. Luke points out that His growth was comprehensive and balanced. His growth in wisdom implies that He grew intellectually. He did not go through all of the processes that were common among the religious leaders of His day. However, that does not suggest that He did not receive a basic education or that He was not studious. His growth in stature implies that He matured physically. Who better than Jesus would understand that the body is the temple of the Holy Spirit? The fact that He "increased . . . in favor with people" illustrates His social growth. Jesus was a people person! Luke also points out that He grew in favor with God. Jesus grew spiritually and had an intimate relationship with God, the Father. A leader who fails to grow and develop socially, intellectually, physically, or spiritually cannot possibly imitate the growth of Christ, since this is

---

1. Robert H. Stein, *Luke* (New American Commentary 24; Nashville: Broadman & Holman, 1992), 123.

the core description of what He did for eighteen years of His life while preparing for His public ministry.

Growth Principle #1—You must be determined to grow socially, intellectually, and physically as well as spiritually in order to be the leader God wants you to be.

Jesus interacted with God through weekly group worship experiences

> He came to Nazareth, where He had been brought up. As usual, He entered the synagogue on the Sabbath day and stood up to read. (Luke 4:16 HCSB)

It was the custom or the habit of Jesus to attend the synagogue each Sabbath day or each week. Jesus attended worship there every week where He interacted with God and other Jewish worshippers in a *large group* setting. Luke implied that the ruler of the synagogue invited Jesus to read and comment on the Scriptures.[2] The invitation reinforces the fact that Jesus had grown spiritually. His commitment to attend weekly implies that He was devoted and disciplined.

What does this teach about the growth and leadership of Jesus? His consistency and commitment are evidence that He was a person of devotion. Discipline is an important characteristic of a leader. Followers will not exceed the level of commitment or discipline of the leader. The importance of worship is communicated for the spiritual leader. If regular participation in worship was important to the development and leadership of Jesus, the Son of God, how much more important should it be assumed for other spiritual leaders? A dynamic exists when worshipping with a large group that is difficult to duplicate in

---

2. Ibid., 154.

a small group setting. The setting ordinarily includes an insightful and learned leader who teaches and challenges the audience to understand and apply God's Word.

Growth Principle #2—You must be devoted to large group worship experiences to maximize your spiritual growth.

Jesus interacted with God through personal devotion

> Yet He often withdrew to deserted places and prayed. (Luke 5:16 HCSB)

In His worship experiences, Jesus saw leadership in action. The lessons were positive and negative alike as He learned from the religious leaders of His day. An advantage exists in observing and hearing others. A spiritual dynamic is also in play as the participant in worship hears what God says to and through others. God's Word through others can be inspirational and enlightening, but Jesus did not rely on others exclusively to hear a word from God.

Jesus spent time alone with God. He heard directly from God the Father, and He looked to His Father for leadership. Nothing could interrupt the time that was predesignated, set aside, and honored.[3] He often spent time alone with God. Luke's words "often withdrew" emphasize that this was a regular practice of Jesus.[4] The greatest influence on the growth of Jesus and His leadership style is found in this passage. His growth was based on the intimate relationship that He had with God. Anyone can attend a worship service and appear to be engaged, interested, and growing. There is no guarantee

---

3. Laurie Beth Jones, *Jesus, CEO: Using Ancient Wisdom for Visionary Leadership* (New York: Hyperion, 2009), 12.
4. Stein, *Luke*, 173.

that a person in worship is maturing. However, personal time alone with God is difficult to fake. No one is observing. It is between God and the individual. The private time alone with God is what gave Jesus the strength to tackle the public challenges. He reminded the disciples of this important lesson once when they had unsuccessfully tried to drive out a demon (Mark 9:29; cf. Matt. 17:21). The leadership style of Jesus was inside out. In the Sermon on the Mount, He taught that what happens in the heart is what is most important. In regard to leadership, the leader's private life will influence his or her public leadership. The greatest growth comes when you hear from God personally and directly.

Growth Principle #3—You must be disciplined in spending time alone with God to maximize your growth.

Jesus interacted with God within a small group

> During those days He went out to the mountain to pray and spent all night in prayer to God. When daylight came, He summoned His disciples, and He chose 12 of them—He also named them apostles. (Luke 6:12–13 HCSB)

Jesus understood the importance of worship and interacting with God in a large group setting. He also understood how critical it is to spend time alone with God in order to grow and do God's will. Jesus also knew how powerful the dynamics of meeting in a small group can be. Here is where His leadership begins to be evidenced and put into practice. The small group is a place to build intimate relationships. A group of twelve is a setting in which interaction and personal training can take place. Issues can be discussed, questions can be asked, accountability can be implemented, and personal relationships can be developed. It is difficult to accomplish these tasks in a large group and impossible when a person is alone. The small group is perhaps the place where Jesus exerted the greatest amount of influence as He provided leadership.

"His disciples" refers to a larger group of Jesus' followers, who have already been mentioned in Luke 6:1. From this group the Twelve were chosen.[5] Jesus was often seen ministering to the multitudes and preaching to the crowds. Out of the crowd He intentionally organized a small group to instruct and develop. Verses 14–16 of Luke 6 list the Twelve by name. Jesus not only inspired others but also directly enlisted and in essence enrolled them into a small group. He not only excited people; he got them to sign up. He asked his staff out loud and often, "Will you follow me?"[6]

The leadership style of Jesus included personal interaction in large group settings and in small group settings. It is in this small group setting that Jesus began to exercise and model leadership skills that were observable and transferable.

Growth Principle #4—You must be dedicated to a small group to maximize your growth.

CONNECTING THE (GROWTH) DOTS

You will find no substitute for spending personal time with God. It is awesome when you spend time in prayer and the study of God's Word and hear His voice. The opportunity to gather with other believers to worship the God you love magnifies the experience. Praising Him alongside other Christians is inspiring and uplifting. A gifted pastor shares insights that you may have never considered, and your growth increases. Connecting with others is also important. Relationships are the source of ministry, fellowship, and accountability. Meeting in a small group, such as

---

5. Ibid., 192.
6. Jones, *Jesus, CEO*, 240.

a Sunday school class, provides a boost that can propel your spiritual growth to a greater level. Taking joy in social, intellectual, and physical growth opportunities enhances your connection with others as well as with the God who created you. You need the balance that Jesus modeled as well as a comprehensive approach to growth and interaction with God if you are to lead others to do likewise. Follow the example of Jesus and lead others to do so as well.

One of the results of spiritual growth is leadership or influence over others. As the Gospel of Luke proceeds, the reader can observe a pattern of leadership that Jesus used to lead others to grow and serve. Is that not ultimately what a Sunday school leader should be doing? How can you lead others to grow and serve?

Jesus summoned others to join him

> During those days He went out to the mountain to pray and spent all night in prayer to God. When daylight came, He summoned His disciples, and He chose twelve of them—He also named them apostles. (Luke 6:12–13 HCSB)

Did you notice that Jesus called a small group out of a larger group? He did not present a message and ask people to sign up for the group. He did not make an announcement before a larger group inviting people to join on a first come, first serve basis. He prayed to God and determined whom He should approach. He went to them directly and asked them to follow Him. It was a great compliment to the apostles to know that Jesus had prayed and that God had placed each of them personally on His heart to be a part of His team.

The group described in the verses that follow was not a loose coalition of followers. As noted earlier, all twelve are listed by name. He ministered to hundreds and even thousands. However, He poured His life into a specific group of twelve over a three-year period. I do not want to read too much into the number "twelve" at this point. I want to emphasize the first step that Jesus took in leading the apostles through a growth process. The key point here is that He intentionally and directly enlisted them to be a part of the group. What is the equivalent practice for a Sunday school leader?

Do you have a class roster or Sunday school roll? Perhaps the people on the roll were assigned to you or were inherited from a previous leader. I would not assume that any of them are on the list by accident. Begin with the premise that God has placed them under your leadership by His divine design. Here is a key question: Is there someone, perhaps more than one, who should be on that list? Have you prayed and asked God about others who should be in your group? Jesus prayed and directly enlisted people to be a part of His group. The equivalent in Sunday school is to enroll them in the class. Enlisting or enrolling them is the first step in a process of leading them to maximize their spiritual growth.

Leadership Principle #1—You must pray and directly enlist people to be a part of your small group.

Jesus took responsibility for their spiritual growth

> Soon afterward He was traveling from one town and village to another, preaching and telling the good news of the Kingdom of God. The Twelve were with Him. (Luke 8:1 HCSB)

What should happen after they are enlisted? It is not coincidental that the apostles were with Jesus as He went about preaching and teaching. Jesus had specifically asked them to follow Him. As you read the Gospels, you see Jesus taking opportunities to instruct the apostles as He modeled a healthy relationship with the Father. They were not meeting at 9:45 every Sunday morning, but they were meeting together frequently, receiving instruction from Jesus, asking and answering questions, learning to minister to the needs of others, praying together, and growing in their relationship with God in spite of many personal failures and setbacks.

Jesus did not take a passive approach to the spiritual development of the men He had enlisted. He spent time with them in order to help them grow in their relationship with God while teaching them to minister to the needs of those around them. As you are considering my four principles of leadership, you will notice that they are progressive levels. Jesus enlisted or enrolled them and then began to engage them in the study and application of the Word of God.

The equivalent practice in a Sunday school setting is easy to see at this point. Sunday school leaders are familiar with the concept of teaching God's Word as the class meets together each week. Most Sunday school leaders tend to place a majority of their time and energy on preparation and presentation of a Bible study. Many teachers will go through an entire year (or many years) without ever applying the first principle of praying about and directly enlisting others to be a part of the group as Jesus did. The Sunday school will not grow if others are not invited to become involved. Likewise, many teachers will not move beyond the teaching to apply the additional principles we will consider next. Please note that the heading of this section is not "He took responsibility for teaching His apostles." He took responsibility for their spiritual growth. He did not teach and leave it up to them to apply the Scripture and to grow. He personally engaged and challenged them to live what they learned. His approach was intentional, intense, comprehensive, active, applicable, and personal. That stands in contrast to many Sunday school classes where a teacher shows up just on time, presents an uninspiring lecture, prays, and says, "I'll see you all next week." It is this type of approach that leads people to conclude that Sunday school is irrelevant.

I could not agree more if that were the way a Sunday school class is supposed to be led.

Leadership Principle #2—You must determine how you will engage every member of your group to help them to grow spiritually.

Jesus equipped them to serve

> Summoning the Twelve, He gave them power and authority over all the demons and [power] to heal diseases. (Luke 9:1 HCSB)

The apostles saw Jesus at work in his public ministry and heard Him as He taught others in addition to instructing the apostles directly. They served alongside Jesus as He went to the various towns and villages. Jesus took the apostles outside of a classroom and into the community to apply what they were learning. He modeled for them what it means to love and have compassion on others. At that point He took the group to a greater level of personal growth. They had watched as He cast out demons and healed the sick, and then He equipped them to do likewise.

Jesus gave them what they would need to accomplish the task that He was about to place before them. He was preparing to send them into the community to do the same thing they had observed Him doing. They could not cast out demons or heal the sick without the tools to do so. Jesus knew that the impact on the community could be multiplied if others were equipped to serve, which ultimately would allow them to minister in multiple settings simultaneously.

Nothing more than teaching will occur unless the members are equipped to serve and to exercise their spiritual gifts. What is the point of teaching if application never moves from theoretical to actual? Jesus not only taught the apostles what they should do but also took the extra step to make sure they were equipped to do it. Do you want your class members to minister to one another? You must equip them to do it. Do you want your class to be friendly to guests? You must equip them to do it. Do you want your class to be strong in prayer? You must equip them to do it. Equipping ordinarily involves an organizational component. For example, you will be hard pressed to find a class that ministers consistently and comprehensively unless care group leaders (or an equivalent type of ministry) are enlisted, organized, and equipped to minister to a group. Unless ongoing accountability is added, it is likely to fizzle within a few months. Jesus equipped the apostles and sent them out. As you study the Scripture, you will note that they came back to report what they had experienced.

I stated earlier that a Sunday school that works is one where the lost are reached, lives are changed, and leaders are sent. Why do many Sunday school classes fail to reach out to the lost and unchurched? The teacher often does not teach it nor intentionally model it, and no one is equipped to do it. Is it any wonder that many classes go months and even years without seeing anyone come to know Christ? Every class should serve as an equipping station as well as a teaching station if the Sunday school is to really work.

Leadership Principle #3—You must equip the members of your group to serve.

Jesus sent them out to serve

> Then He sent them to proclaim the kingdom of God and to heal the sick. (Luke 9:2 HCSB)

In Luke 8:1 you will recall that Jesus was ministering and

the disciples were with Him. They spent time observing Jesus as He ministered and taught, and as time passed they began to minister alongside Him. He instructed and equipped them to minister to the needs of people and to share the good news. It was at this point that Jesus sent the disciples out to apply what they had learned and experienced in His presence. The first occasion was apparently a test run and a learning experience in and of itself. Verse 10 says: "When the apostles returned, they reported to Jesus all that they had done. He took them alone and withdrew privately to a town called Bethsaida" (HCSB).

Jesus sent His disciples out at this point, but He stayed involved in their lives and ministries. I imagine that they had a lot of questions when they returned. Jesus met with the group privately to debrief and to continue instructing and equipping them to serve effectively. Later, the time came when Jesus released them completely to go out and minister on their own (physically speaking). In Luke 24:50–51, Luke describes the ascension of Jesus into heaven. Matthew, an eyewitness, shares the same account in Matthew 28. It was at that point in time that Jesus gave the Great Commission to His followers. After three years and a few months, Jesus released the apostles from the group (of twelve) and sent them to "make disciples of all nations."

The ultimate aim and the greatest mark of effectiveness of a Sunday school leader can be observed at this point. Jesus extended His influence into the world by equipping and then releasing His disciples to minister outside of the group of twelve. Sunday school teachers should have the same goal. A Sunday school that works is one from which leaders are sent.

Leadership Principle #4—You must extend your influence by releasing leaders to serve outside of your group.

A Sunday school that really works is more than a Bible

study. It is a life-changing experience for the participants. The teacher has a holistic view of ministry and understands that he or she is commissioned to lead a group of followers on a spiritual journey. It is a group into which new people are added and from which established members are released each and every year. The group is challenged to grow in their intimacy with the Father, to work together to act on the (Great) commission of the Son, and to exercise their gifts in the power of the Holy Spirit as they serve and fellowship together. The journey of Jesus' life and leadership is the pattern.

DISCUSSION QUESTIONS

1. How is physical, social, and intellectual growth related to spiritual growth? Do church leaders have responsibility to assist with these components of growth? If so, how?

2. How do large group, small group, and individual spiritual encounters differ in their ability to help people connect with God and grow spiritually? How does your church emphasize each of these types of spiritual disciplines and encounters?

3. In what ways can Sunday school leaders take responsibility for the personal spiritual growth of their members beyond teaching the lesson each week?

4. How often do the classes or small groups in your church purposefully get outside of the classroom to minister together as Jesus did with His disciples? How can this be emphasized and improved with your leaders?

5. How intentional are leaders in your church at growing and then releasing leaders to serve in other areas? How can this be emphasized and improved with your leaders?

CHAPTER 3

The Measure of a Sunday School That Works

A CALL CAME INTO OUR OFFICE some time ago with an interesting question. A lady called to ask our staff if her church was growing. Bear in mind that we have access to statistical information on all of the churches within our state convention. I thought that was a very strange question. I am not sure what her motivation was. I can think of positive and negative reasons for why she would have called our office to ask such a question. Was it not evident to her? I have had the privilege of being a part of several growing churches. I do not personally recall a circumstance where I was unsure of whether the church was growing or not.

WHAT DOES IT MEAN TO GROW?

People struggle with this issue of what it means for the church to grow for a variety of reasons. Some object because they do not think that the church "should be out for numbers." I have observed that these tend to be people from churches that are not reaching the lost. It relieves the pressure that they would feel if any objective measure was given legitimacy. Others object on theological grounds. They have embraced a view that the sovereignty of God excludes the possibility that you or I play any role in others trusting Christ as Savior. While I agree that only God can save by His grace, I also believe that I have a responsibility to be obedient to the Great Commission in proclaiming the gospel and being a witness of what Christ has done in my life. (Do not get stuck at this point. The book that you are reading is not a deliberation on the finer points of theology.) I cannot please God by being passive about the proclamation of the gospel message. Yet some Sunday school leaders sincerely believe that the priority of their ministry is to dive deep into God's Word and to disciple believers to love God intimately. I certainly cannot disagree with the significance of devoted Bible study and loving God, but I have noticed that many go deep and somehow fail to see the lost community around them. I propose that a Sunday school that works seeks growth. But how do you measure growth?

How do you know if your church or your class is growing? Should you compare average worship attendance to the previous year? Sunday school average attendance? Total membership? Sunday school enrollment? Perhaps there is a formula that combines these factors. The problem is that all of these numbers can increase without anyone in the community coming to know Christ as Savior. These are quantitative measurements that have value and can enable the observer to see trends over spans of time, but they do not tell you with certainty that your Sunday school is working.

The First Community Church increased by more than 10 percent in the past year in membership, Sunday school enrollment, average worship attendance, and average Sunday school attendance. On the surface it appears that they had a tremendous amount of growth. However, no unchurched people in the community trusted Christ. All of the baptisms were children and students who attend with their parents and a couple of families who joined from another denomination. The community is rapidly growing, the congregation provides excellent ministry at their facility, and a neighboring church is losing members due to a crisis. Has this church really grown? The numbers have increased but is the Sunday school really working?

The Hope Church in a neighboring community experienced a decrease of more than 10 percent in the past year in membership, Sunday school enrollment, average worship attendance, and Sunday school attendance. They are very evangelistic and were blessed to baptize more this year than in any previous year in the history of their church. Almost half of those baptized were formerly unchurched people who came to know Christ through the ministry and witness of the members. Almost all of those who trusted Christ are involved in a small group or Sunday school class. The church made a bold decision this past year. They intentionally released ten families, some of whom were their strongest leaders, to plant a new church in another part of the community to reach people that the church has not yet affected. Has this church really declined? Is their Sunday school not working?

Your church is not really growing unless the community is being penetrated with the gospel message, people are trusting Christ as their Savior, and the church is taking responsibility to lead them to grow in their personal relationship with Christ. Jesus said: "Go therefore and make disciples of all nations, baptizing them in the name of the Father and of the Son and the Holy Spirit, teaching them to observe all things that I have commanded you; and lo, I am with you always, even to the end of the age" (Matt. 28:19–20).

If a church is effective at accomplishing this commission within the community, the membership and the numbers reflected in the quantitative measurements are likely to increase over time. Some leaders evaluate using a mono-measurement that utilizes a metric intended to reflect effectiveness in evangelism. The premise is that an increase in baptisms is a measure of growth. How many people were baptized in your church last year? That is a good question to begin with, but it does not totally address the issue of effectiveness. A large number of church baptisms are based on biological growth. The baptisms reflect the commitment of the children of existing church members to trust Christ and to follow Him in believer's baptism. For those commitments we are thankful and can rejoice. However, the Great Commission does not command us to sit and watch as we are blessed to see the children of believers follow the pattern of their parents in trusting Christ.

In addition, some of the baptisms are the result of the decisions of active members to rededicate their lives to Christ, to experience scriptural baptism in response to some past error, or to meet a denominational conviction about the mode of baptism. Again, these are legitimate decisions, and the importance of being scripturally baptized cannot be minimized. The point, however, is that a church can baptize ten, twenty, thirty, or more people in a year and not reach any of the lost and unchurched in the community. Faithfully reaching into the community to share the gospel will not have any negative effect on significant commitments within the congregation. However, the growth that I am describing is the result of proclaiming the gospel message inside and outside of the walls of the church, resulting in the formerly unchurched trusting Christ as Savior and being discipled by the local church. One factor that growing churches have in common is a clear focus on evangelism.[1]

I believe that one of the best ways to measure growth and effectiveness is through qualitative measurements. The

---

1. Ken Hemphill, *The Bonsai Theory of Church Growth* (Nashville: Broadman & Holman, 1991), 131.

Sunday school or small groups are the best place to make the evaluation because the impact of the classes or groups has a ripple effect. An increase in membership or worship may or may not affect participation in your Sunday school. However, a growing Sunday school will almost always result in a growing worship attendance, membership, and expansion of almost every ministry within the church. Sunday school growth can drive the growth of worship and membership while enhancing assimilation and involvement in missions. It is certainly possible to identify prominent churches with weak Sunday school ministries. However, it is unlikely, if not impossible, that a church would be weak if they have a strong and healthy Sunday school. Quantitative measurements like Sunday school enrollment and average worship attendance can and often will reflect numerical growth but will not necessarily indicate if the Sunday school is working. These measurements have great value when measuring cumulative growth of the churches in a community, association, or denomination, and they should not be ignored as a tool in analyzing the growth of a local church. However, is there a way a church can look behind those numbers to determine if the Sunday school is really working? The answer is yes, by measuring the quality and nature of growth observed and measured over time. Qualitative measurements are more time intensive but are the best way to evaluate the strength and effectiveness of a Sunday school ministry.

A Sunday school that really works is one where the lost are reached, lives are changed, and leaders are sent. Every Sunday school leader should take time to evaluate his or her effectiveness on a regular basis in these areas. The challenge here is that many leaders will be unwilling to do so. Qualitative measurements take more time and energy on the part of the leaders. It is work. It will result in higher accountability as a result of evaluating the effectiveness of the class. The difficulty with evaluation is that the results are not always positive. It is much easier to roll along week by week, presenting a lesson and hoping for the best rather than honestly evaluating oneself with the prospect of having to grow, improve, or change. It comes down to this: do you really want to be the leader that God has called you to be? If so, you must inspect what you expect. Using qualitative measurements will help you in a couple of ways. You will quickly see where the strengths and weaknesses of the class are in the context of the biblical purpose. That will enable you to understand where to place your energy and emphasis in the coming months. Ultimately, your ministry and leadership will be more balanced, your class will be healthier, and you will be contributing to the growth of the kingdom. The following questions may help you to better apply the strategy that Jesus used in developing the leadership of the apostles. Are you ready?

Are the lost being reached?

- How many members of my class/group have shared his or her faith with someone in the past three months?

- Has our class participated in an activity/project/mission in the last four months with the express purpose of sharing the gospel with a group in our community and seeing people trust Christ as Savior?

- Is there someone in our class/group who trusted Christ and was baptized within the past twelve months?

Alternate questions for leaders of preschool and younger children:

- Have we partnered with any adult classes to provide

childcare to free them up to engage in evangelistic opportunities in the past four months?

- Are we purposefully reaching out to unchurched preschoolers and children to lay a foundation for a gospel response and to see parents come to know Christ?

Are lives being changed?

- How many members of my class/group are committed to interact with God through personal devotion, small group participation, and large group worship experiences on a regular basis?

- How many of my members participated in missions and ministry projects in the community this past year?

- How many members of my class have I conducted an interview with this year to determine their spiritual progress and spiritual needs?

Alternate questions for leaders of preschool and younger children:

- Have I learned and am I committed to applying sound instruction based on the maturity level of my class, or am I focused on babysitting?

- Do I pray for the spiritual development of my class and for the spiritual climate of their homes regularly?

- Do I regularly contact parents of those who do not attend church to encourage and motivate them to prioritize their families' involvement in small group Bible study?

Are leaders being sent?

- How many members of my class/group have been identified and equipped to serve in a ministry/missions role?

- How many members of my class/group have participated in an evangelism or ministry activity/project/mission in the past twelve months?

- How many members of my class/group have I released to serve outside of the class in the past twelve months?

Alternate questions for leaders of preschool, children, and youth:

- Have I made the commitment and sacrifice to be with my group every week to maximize my effectiveness in ministry (as opposed to rotating every couple of weeks)?

- Have I enlisted at least one person in the past year to serve alongside of me?

- Has our class participated in an evangelism or ministry activity/project/mission in the past twelve months?

What would your class (and church) be like if you could answer each of these questions in the affirmative? It would be absolutely amazing! These questions are not perfect. Not only would I not object, but also I would encourage you to sharpen the questions and take time to evaluate your class or classes. I would encourage you not to add a lot of additional questions. Once you address these nine you will have your hands full. It may be that you are blown away by reading these questions.

Don't be overwhelmed! You may be thinking right now that you want to "go back to Egypt" like the Hebrews did when the scouts brought back their report from the reconnaissance in the Promised Land. It would be easier to lead your class like you always have and let the chips fall where they may. However, God has called you to something greater. He wants you to lead your class to be a place where the lost are being reached, lives are being changed, and leaders are being sent. That is where you want to take your Sunday school class. It will take time. It will take effort. It will never work out perfectly because it is a journey. Part of getting to where you need to go is by knowing exactly where you are. If you go online to MapQuest to find directions, you will be asked two questions: where do you want to go (your destination), and where are you departing from (your current location)? Taking the time to evaluate what you're doing by using these questions will remind you of your destination and give you a clear view of your current location.

You can use these questions in a couple of ways. You may answer them yourself using educated estimations based on the relationship that you have with class members and data that you have at hand. What are your strengths and weaknesses? What do you need to work on with your class? Surveying your class would probably give you a clearer picture. You may want to begin the new Sunday school year by giving your class a pretest and then administering it again every six months to measure progress (see appendix A). The most challenging issue to get your arms around in regard to these questions is the issue of "lives being changed." It is difficult to quantify what is going on in a person's heart. I submit that asking a third question is the key: how many members of my class have I conducted an interview with this year to determine their spiritual progress and spiritual needs? Yes, it calls for a sacrifice of time and is time intensive. I challenge you to annually interview every member or couple in your class to get a sense of their spiritual needs and spiritual progress. I propose that some of you who do so will have the privilege of seeing someone come to know Christ through this process. The interview should preferably be conducted by the teacher but could be done by group leaders if the class is larger. In that case the teacher needs to meet with the group leaders following the interviews for a time of debriefing. You will find a sample questionnaire and some suggested guidelines in appendix B.

If you conduct a survey of your class using qualitative measurements, you will probably be discouraged initially. The aim is not to depress you but to challenge you. You will find that with all of your prayer, energy, and effort, the results may still be disappointing even five and ten years later. Remember that the disciples had Jesus as their leader and they struggled throughout their growth process. The reason for investing time in evaluation is that you want all of your class/group members to be growing, serving, and sharing their faith. The reality is that you will always have members who are struggling, uncommitted, and unresponsive. I love to play golf, although I never shoot par. I do have occasional holes where I succeed, but my cumulative score never measures up. I do not really compete against others. My aim is always to improve my game and to improve my score. Even though I do not shoot par, taking three or four strokes off of my game is a great improvement. You will not likely ever get all of your class/group members to the point where they are growing, serving, and sharing, but leading two or three more members to grow, serve, and share can make a huge difference in your class, your church, and even your community. Use the measurements as a baseline to move forward in helping your class to grow.

THE RELEVANCE OF NUMBERS

Do you recall the parable of the lost sheep in Luke 15:1–7? Of the one hundred sheep in the flock there was one missing. How did the shepherd know? Evidently he counted. If he did not count, he may have never noticed that the sheep was missing, and it may have been lost forever. However, the shepherd's awareness of the missing sheep motivated him to take action. He left the ninety-nine in the wilderness and pursued the one that was lost. You recall how the sheep was found and the rejoicing that took place with the shepherd's friends and neighbors as well as in heaven over the one sinner who repents. Counting does have a place and can make a difference.

The reason for counting is not because we should be concerned with "numbers." Ministry is about people and relationships. Our aim is to connect people to Jesus Christ and to help them develop an intimate relationship with Him. Numbers are simply a tool. They can be useful in evaluation and can help you as a leader to identify strengths and weaknesses. In turn you can adjust your focus or improve in some area that will enable you and your congregation or class to be more effective in ministering to people and connecting them to Christ. I trust that you want to maximize your potential in touching as many lives as possible while you have the opportunity.

You can learn a lot about your Sunday school class and church from numbers (quantitative measurements). Numbers do not tell the whole story, but they can give you a quick snapshot. For example, a decline in attendance may indicate a problem, but it does not tell you what the problem is. An increase in attendance can be encouraging, but it does not indicate whether the church is reaching the lost unless other questions are pursued. What should you count and how can you use the numbers to strengthen your class and church? The first two of the following items are also included in the quantitative measurements previously discussed.

Baptisms

How many people in the class have come into a relationship with Christ and have been baptized in the past year? (This question does not apply to younger children and preschool classes.) You will discover very quickly whether or not the lost are being reached by asking and answering this question. The fact that they are in the class or group also indicates that the discipleship process has begun.

Leaders Released

How many class members have we released to serve in other areas or to start new classes in the past year? Here is why this question is important: where do preschool teachers come from? The answer is, from adult Sunday school classes. Where do you find leaders for children's ministry? How about student ministry leaders? Do you see the pattern here? They all come from adult classes. The entire church is counting on adult classes to equip and release members to serve in their ministry areas. The number of leaders who are equipped and released from your class is perhaps the greatest measure of your effectiveness as a teacher. You may have a smaller attendance than one year ago but be contributing more to the growth of the body. Do not be selfish with your leaders. You have not been commissioned to hoard members but to equip and send them to serve the body of Christ.

Enrollment

What is the total number of people currently enrolled in your class, and how does it compare with Labor Day weekend? The current enrollment should be higher unless you have released a large number to start a new class since that weekend. The greater number is an indicator that your class is seeking to minister to a greater number of people and that you are assimilating those who have come to know Christ as Savior. In addition, you will discover as you read further that the enrollment affects your attendance and your ability to minister to your entire congregation.

Number of Guests Present

How many guests have attended your class in the past month? A Sunday school class is intended to be an open group. An open group meets weekly for Bible study throughout the year and can be visited or joined at any point. It is open to nonbelievers and nonmembers as well as Christians and members. You are not likely to have guests every week (although that would be ideal). However, a lack of any guests may reveal a potential problem. It is usually an indicator that the class members have lost sight of or do not understand the purpose of the class, or that the class is boring. In any case, the teacher should take action. It is not a call to resign but a call to improve.

Contacts Made

How many ministry contacts have been made by the class in the past week? A contact is an intentional communication on behalf of the Sunday school class through phone calls, e-mails, visits, cards, social networking, or wayside encounters. The purpose of the communication can vary from invitations to participate, follow-up of guests, ministry to members, encouragement to sporadic attendees, or any ministry need that a class has responsibility for. It can only be assumed that no ministry is taking place if there are no contacts to report.

Attendance

What has the average attendance been for the past month? Attendance may be higher or lower on any given Sunday due to seasonal ebb and flow. In addition, you will have members each week who are out of town, sick, or dealing with family emergencies as well as some who vary in their level of commitment. It is encouraging when the attendance is higher and is increasing. Whether the attendance is increasing, decreasing, or remaining static, you should not be afraid to ask why. The answer may help you to be more effective in ministering to and reaching others in the future.

WHAT TO DO WHEN ATTENDANCE IS DOWN

It is so easy to get discouraged when the Sunday school attendance drops. Most Sunday school leaders have a desire to provide leadership for a committed group that reaches out and is blessed to receive guests and new believers on a regular basis. What do you do when there is a disconnect between your desire and the results? Keep in mind that you have very little control over how many people attend on a given Sunday, similar to your lack of control over the weather. The temperature is going to be what it is going to be. That is in God's control. However, just because it is thirty-two degrees outside does not mean that you have to be cold. You have control of some factors. You choose whether or not to wear a coat and gloves. You choose whether to spend the night outside or inside. You choose the setting for your thermostat. Even if it is thirty-two degrees outside you can be comfortable if you make the appropriate choices.

How does the weather relate to your Sunday school? Focus on what you can control instead of what you cannot control. For example, you can choose whether or not to participate in or provide training. I have discovered that churches that provide training are generally growing and those that do not are generally declining. Research conducted in our state of Georgia revealed that churches that provided training at least four times a year grew their average Sunday school attendance by 12.4 percent over three years. However, churches that provided no training declined by 2.1 percent over the same time span (see table 3.1).[2] Likewise, you can also choose whether or not

---

2. Tom Crites, "Sunday School/Open Group Ministry: A Look at Statistics Related to Sunday School" (Atlanta: GBC Research, 2004), previously available at gabaptist.org.

to enroll someone new in Sunday school on any given week. If your church enrolled one additional person each week, the result would be an increase of about fifty people enrolled. A class that does a good job of ministry to its members can expect half of those enrolled to be present on average. The choice of several leaders to enroll new members could potentially result in as many as twenty-five additional people attending in future weeks.

Table 3.1. Sunday School Leadership Question Results from 2002 Annual Church Profile						
Frequency of Leadership Training	Number of Churches	Churches in Each Training Category (%)	Average Sunday School Attendance		
			1999	2002	% Change
Weekly	88	3.5	20,430	21,725	+ 6.3
Monthly	202	7.9	59,999	68,045	+13.4
Quarterly	314	12.3	46,569	53,004	+13.8
Annually	540	21.2	64,482	67,167	+ 4.2
Other frequency	367	14.4	37,107	37,412	+ 0.8
Never	1,033	40.6	47,733	46,727	- 2.1
Total*	2,544	100.0			

Source: Table has been abbreviated from Research Services, Georgia Baptist Convention, February 2003.
*There were 2,544 of 3,008 churches that responded to the leadership question: "How often do you conduct Sunday school leadership training?"

You control whether to start a new class this year or not. A new class usually reaches people that existing classes have been unable to reach. You also have control over how many contacts you make and how many people you invite to Sunday school. Why do guests attend? The answer: because they are invited. The number of total contacts made influences week-to-week attendance about as much as any other factor. You also have control over whether or not to provide a fellowship to reach out to guests and to enhance the relationships of the attendees. You also have control over the discovery of a new prospect or the follow-up of a first-time guest. You do have control over many actions, but none of them make a great impact in and of themselves.

The cumulative effect of doing these things (and the above list is not comprehensive) is at best an increase in attendance and at worst more stability in attendance. Keep one other thing in mind. The temperature does not remain at thirty-two degrees forever, unless you are near the Arctic. Your Sunday school is prone to seasons of better attendance in August, September, October, January, and February as well as seasons of struggle in November, December, April, June, and July. (These may vary in your part of the world.) Always evaluate by comparing the total average attendance of all classes for the entire month with the same month one year ago. Your attendance may be down from last month but way up from one year ago. In summary, focus on the principles that drive the growth, and with God's blessing the attendance will follow! Learning about a Sunday school that really works will help you in establishing and practicing those principles.

WHO IS RESPONSIBLE FOR THE GROWTH OF YOUR CLASS?

"I planted, Apollos watered, but God gave the growth" (1 Cor. 3:6). Apparently there was some contention in the Corinthian church about who was responsible for the growth. Is growth the result of a relevant and effective strategy conceived by man? Is it the result of a leader with a charismatic personality? Or is it an outpouring of God unrelated to any human participation?

I moved into a new home a couple years ago. The builder installed Bermuda sod in my front yard, and I had it installed in the back shortly after moving in. I did not plant it. Someone else did. I believe in the sovereignty of God. If He were to remove His hand from my yard, it would not have life and would have no chance of living. God sends the rain, and my grass lives only by His grace. He has assigned a role to me to help in the process. I have responsibility for fertilizing it, keeping it watered, and cutting and trimming it. If I do not do my part, I will not have a lawn that is healthy or growing. Someone else planted it, I care for (water) it, but God grows it. I do have a role to play in the process, but I do not cause my grass to grow.

It may be that you did not start or plant your class, and I believe that only God can grow it, but as a Sunday school teacher you do have a role in the process. You must learn how to fertilize, water, and cut and trim your class. Pray that God will never remove His hand from it. Humanly speaking, you do have responsibility. Church (class) growth is a supernatural activity accomplished by God through human instrumentation.[3] You are the instrument that God wants to use to grow your class. The responsibility of the teacher is to lead.

The pastor and staff also have responsibility. Ephesians 4:11–16 is perhaps the most descriptive passage in the Bible about the strategic elements of church growth. Verse 16 concludes the theme of the passage with the statement "causes the growth of the body." What body is Paul referring to? He is referring to the body of Christ, that is, the church.

In Ephesians 4:1, Paul encourages every believer to "walk worthy of the calling with which you were called." He assumes that each believer is a part of the body (or team) and that each person has responsibility. The words *calling* and *called* imply that God has given every person an assignment. Ignoring or neglecting the responsibility is not an option. Since God is the recruiter who has called them to their place of service, they

---

3. Ibid., 53.

should serve in a manner befitting the One who called or enlisted them.

God makes provision for each believer to fulfill his or her responsibilities in two ways. First, He gives each person one or more spiritual gifts that enable the person to fulfill his or her roles. Paul states: "But to each one of us grace was given according to the measure of Christ's gift" (Eph. 4:7). Paul more comprehensively addresses the issue of spiritual gifts in Romans 12 and 1 Corinthians 12. He told the Corinthians that the "one and same Spirit works all things, distributing to each one individually as He wills" (1 Cor. 12:11) and that "the manifestation of the Spirit is given to each one for the profit of all" (1 Cor. 12:7). Every Christian is called to service, gifted to serve, and has a gift that contributes to the health and growth of the body (church).

Second, God gives leaders in the church to equip believers for the work of ministry so the body of Christ is built up and grows toward maturity. The emphasis in 1 Corinthians 12 and Romans 12 is on spiritual gifts assigned to believers. The emphasis in Ephesians 4 is on the resources of leadership that God places within the church. Church leaders are in place to help people exercise and utilize their gifts so every believer can "walk worthy of [his or her] calling." The gifts that the Spirit gives are external to the believer as well as internal. Pastors and staff are the external gifts given to believers (Eph. 4:11) to enable them to fulfill their responsibilities through exercise of their internal spiritual gifts.

The passage specifically mentions the pastor, and the application is direct. Pastors bear responsibility for training the members for ministry, including those who are called to lead the Sunday school ministry. The Scripture never specifically instructs pastors regarding the conducting of weddings or funerals, though they would do well to perform these as a courtesy and a ministry to the members. However, pastors do have specific instructions to train their members for ministry. The point of Ephesians 4:11–12 is that pastors have been placed in the church specifically with that aim in mind. In fact, the Greek word *katartismos* ("training, preparing, or equipping") in verse 12 conveys the idea of a harmonious development in which all parts are brought to a condition of being able to perform according to their created purpose.[4]

The pastor also receives a benefit when he follows the instruction to equip believers. He cannot and should not do all of the ministry alone. The Sunday school provides an avenue to distribute the responsibility to minister to all of the members. Every believer is called to serve and to minister inside and outside of the body of Christ. He has gifted believers for that purpose. Even a small church of fewer than fifty members can accomplish more when every believer serves than a larger church where the pastor is doing most of the ministry all by himself. When a pastor equips members for ministry, including those who lead the Sunday school, he has a team of leaders to assist him in accomplishing the mission and purpose of the church. A team, all members playing their part, can accomplish more together than an individual can alone.

Every pastor has a challenging task. The Scripture mandates that they equip their members for ministry. Planning and announcing an evening of training will not be sufficient for the task. The pastor must take the lead by strategically planning opportunities for equipping the members. He must seek ways to equip through modeling, preaching, and teaching as well as by strategically training his congregation. He must use his skills to motivate, inspire, and encourage the participation of the members in training. He may need to participate in equipping opportunities for himself in order to be an effective equipper. The pastor and

---

4. Arthur G. Patzia, *Ephesians, Colossians, Philemon* (New International Biblical Commentary 10; Peabody, MA: Hendrickson, 1990), 243.

staff must do what it takes in order to fulfill the responsibility laid out in Ephesians 4:11–16. The rewards for obeying the instruction in this passage from God's Word are great. To neglect the training of church members and leaders for service is not an option. The responsibility of the pastor and staff is to understand what causes the growth of the body and to provide the equipping needed for leaders to effectively fulfill their roles. The responsibility of the Sunday school teacher is to receive the equipping and to apply the principles learned as he or she leads others. In summary, God grows the Sunday school, but pastors, staff, teachers, and members are His tools. You have a responsibility to understand the principles of growth and to allow God to use you as His instrument in the growth of the body.

What are the tools that you will need? The foundation has been laid as we have considered the relevance of Sunday school, considered the growth and leadership journey of Jesus as a model, and wrestled with the best ways to measure effectiveness. It begins on the inside, in the heart, and flows outward into practices that are biblically based and experientially proven. Let's proceed to discover how it is that a church can have a Sunday school that really works.

DISCUSSION QUESTIONS

1. In what ways have you been measuring the health and growth of your Sunday school ministry?

2. How can quantitative measures assist in evaluating the strengths and weaknesses of your Sunday school?

3. How can qualitative measures assist in evaluating the strengths and weaknesses of your Sunday school? Are there

qualitative measures mentioned in this chapter that you have neglected to consider in the past?

4. How do you measure "lives being changed"?

5. How do you need to adjust your approach to measuring the effectiveness of your Sunday school?

CHAPTER 4

A Sunday School That Really _W_ORKS . . .

W_ants to_
G_row_

IMAGINE A SUNDAY SCHOOL CLASS where the lost are being reached, lives are being changed, and leaders are being sent. All of the members of the class would be blessed, and they would certainly be a blessing to others. The connection and consistency that the class would have with the Great Commission would be pleasing to God, and the participants would have a positive impact on both their congregation and the community. You might assume at an initial glance that this would be the aim of every Sunday school leader. I regret, however, to admit that it is not the case. In Numbers 14 you will discover that the Hebrews were being led by Moses into the Promised Land. They had been delivered from bondage (four hundred years of slavery), delivered from their enemies, delivered from hunger and thirst, and a great opportunity lay ahead. Twelve men were selected to go ahead of the group to scout out the land and to report what it would take to move forward. Ten of the twelve reported that the land was fertile and fruitful but that there were enemies who would oppose and perhaps defeat them. It was at that point that the people made an amazing statement: "Let's appoint a[nother] leader and go back to Egypt" (Num. 14:4 HCSB). Can you believe that? God had delivered them, brought them to this point, and promised that He would give them the land. Granted it would be hard work, require some sacrifices, and would not necessarily be a comfortable endeavor. They said in essence that it was not worth the sacrifices that it would require. They apparently were not sure that God would grant them victory, and they argued that they would prefer not to go. What was God's response? He said that they would never see the land (Num. 14:23–24). He did not make them go. The Great Commission commands us to "go" and make disciples, and He concludes by saying that He will be with us until the end of the age. Unfortunately, some people do not want to go.

A grandfather was regaling his grandchildren with exploits from his military service. He explained that he had served in the armed forces as a paratrooper. "How many jumps did you make, Granddad?" asked one of his grandchildren. "None," he replied. Another child asked, "How can you say you were a paratrooper if you never jumped?" He responded, "Oh, I never jumped, but I was pushed over forty times!" The task of the paratrooper is to jump. The task of the Sunday school leader is to engage the followers in fulfilling the Great Commission. Too many classes meet in the plane and enjoy the flight, but they never make the leap. Leading a class to have a Great Commission focus requires doing battle with the enemy (and sadly, sometimes with the members) and making sacrifice that sometimes inconveniences members. I challenge you to identify a class or a church where the lost are being reached, lives are being changed, and leaders are being sent that does so without taking on these discomforts. It may be that God has called you to give your leaders or your classes a holy push into the realm of Great Commission skydiving.

It is easy to spiritualize and justify failure in order to give the appearance of having a Great Commission focus. You may think, "As long as I love Jesus it will all work out." Others may propose, "You just need to faithfully teach God's Word, and He will do the rest." I wholeheartedly agree that teachers should love Jesus (with all of their heart, mind, soul, and strength) and that they should teach God's Word. The reality is that most Sunday school teachers do love God and do teach His Word, but often the lost are not being reached, lives are not being changed, and leaders are not being sent. There is a leadership dynamic that works in concert with God's blessing and results in growth. Who delivered the Hebrews from bondage in Egypt? Was it God or was it Moses? It was absolutely God. But notice that God used a human leader as an instrument to get the people to move. Moses played an important role, and he wanted to see the people freed and to lead them to the Promised Land.

WHY SHOULD YOU WANT YOUR CLASS TO GROW?

We should all want what's best for our Sunday school classes and small groups, and most of us will agree that we should want them to grow. But why do we want growth, and what kind of growth should we want? In other words, do we want to see our classes growing for the right reasons? Growth in numbers without growth in quality tends to produce symbolism over substance and is usually unsustainable. Growth in quality without growth in numbers is perhaps better but raises other questions that require prayerful attention. There are several reasons you should want your class to grow, and knowing that these are the right reasons helps us stay on track or get back on track when we've veered off course.

As a Response to Christ's Command

And Jesus came and spoke to them saying, "All authority has been given to Me in heaven and on earth. Go therefore and make disciples of all the nations, baptizing them in the name of the Father and of the Son and of the Holy Spirit, teaching them to observe all things that I have commanded you; and lo, I am with you always, even to the end of the age." (Matt. 28:18–20)

In the Great Commission we have the parting instructions of Jesus prior to His ascension into heaven. It is not an apostolic commission, a pastoral commission, or a commission to church staff. The words have been preserved in Holy Scripture because they are as relevant today as when they were spoken. These are the words of Christ to you. The Great Commission is not about your Sunday school class, but your Sunday school class should be about the Great Commission. Growth is a response and a reflection of your obedience to the command of the Great Commission. Obedience to the Great Commission, not church growth, is the appropriate goal for any church (or class). Church growth results from obedience to the Great Commission.[1]

In Order to Follow the Example of Christ

Now it came to pass in those days that He went out to the mountain to pray, and continued all night in prayer to God. And when it was day, He called His disciples to Himself; and from them He chose twelve whom He also named apostles. . . . And after these things the Lord appointed seventy others also. (Luke 6:12–16; 10:1a)

The four Gospels give a thorough account of the relationship that Jesus had with the twelve apostles. Soon thereafter he enlists seventy others. The Bible does not give evidence

---

1. Hemphill, *Revitalizing the Sunday Morning Dinosaur*, 35.

that they were as closely associated with Christ as the Twelve, but it is clear that they were devoted followers, that they were equipped by Jesus, and that He sent them out into the community to minister and share the good news. Why didn't He rely solely on the Twelve for this work? The needs of the community were too great and the work was more than twelve could accomplish. Jesus enlisted followers, engaged them in spiritual growth, equipped them to serve, and extended His ministry by releasing them to serve in the community. He did not limit Himself to the Twelve but purposefully took others through the process also.

For the Joy That Growth Brings

And when he has found [the lost sheep], he lays it on his shoulders, rejoicing. And when he comes home, he calls together his friends and neighbors, saying to them, "Rejoice with me, for I have found my sheep which was lost!" I say to you that likewise there will be more joy in heaven over one sinner who repents than over ninety-nine just persons who need no repentance. (Luke 15:5–7)

Do you enjoy seeing people come to know Christ? Do you enjoy seeing lives changed? That is the ultimate aim of growth. Growth is the result of seeing people come into a growing relationship with Jesus. God desires for people to come into a personal relationship with Him by faith in Jesus, and He gives us the wonderful privilege of being involved in the process of connecting people to Him. Many Sunday school classes are inwardly focused on the nine or nineteen present instead of praying and reaching out to one who is lost. They do not get to experience the joy of the lost being found because they do not join God in the redemptive process. Only God can save, but He gives us the privilege of sharing the good news with others. It is a thrilling experience to be used by God as an individual or as a group to see the person that is lost come into a living relationship with God.

Josh Hunt is experienced in helping Sunday schools to grow. He is a practitioner and author who speaks to hundreds of Sunday school leaders each year. In his book *Double Your Class in Two Years or Less*, he says:

> There are numerous theories about church growth, with as many exceptions as there are principles. In fact, one of the cardinal principles of church growth is that every principle has an exception. Every principle except this one: In order to grow, you must want to grow. Very seldom will sustained growth occur without desire. We may not agree exactly on how to grow a class, but we can agree on this: A class ought to grow. This is the necessary starting point.
>
> This desire must become very personal. You must be highly committed to wanting your group to grow. You should have a deep conviction that says, "My class ought to grow!"[2]

WHY DO "SOME" SUNDAY SCHOOLS GROW?

A view from a distance may lead one to assume that all Sunday schools are alike. They include many common features such as meeting on Sunday morning prior to worship, being held in rooms at the church, having a teacher with a group between five and twenty-five, having classes divided by age groupings, being centered on Bible study, and meeting for about an hour. The similarities do not end there. You would think if all Sunday schools were basically the same, they would be getting the same results. Why is the Sunday school at one

---

2. Josh Hunt, *Your Class Can Double in Two Years or Less* (Loveland, CO: Group Publishing, 1997), 61.

church flourishing while it is struggling at another church just around the corner?

Upon deeper reflection you will often discover that the church with the growing Sunday school has tapped into some principles that the struggling church has not. A 2001 study of the fastest growing Sunday schools in the Georgia Baptist Convention unveiled some interesting results. The fastest growing Sunday schools were identified based on growth in enrollment, average attendance, and baptisms over a five-year span. Baptisms were included as a criterion to ensure that the churches were experiencing evangelistic growth as opposed to transfer growth. The churches identified were in all regions of the state and represented all sizes. They accounted for 1.3 percent of the total Southern Baptist church population in Georgia. Interestingly, these 1.3 percent of churches accounted for 15 percent of the baptisms and 42 percent of the total growth in Sunday school attendance in the state when the survey was conducted.[3]

A survey of these churches revealed ten common practices or characteristics that are not necessarily common to every Sunday school. The fastest growing churches had implemented on average nine of the ten practices. A comparison study of a random group of other Southern Baptist churches in Georgia revealed that other "growing" Sunday schools practiced on average eight of ten. By contrast, those that were in decline or had plateaued practiced an average of fewer than five of the ten. The ten common practices of the fastest growing Sunday schools were as follows:

- 98 percent of the churches with the fastest growing Sunday schools involved their Sunday school leaders in training

---

3. Parr, "Georgia's Fastest Growing Sunday Schools."

- 96 percent viewed their pastor's support of the Sunday school as important to the health of their church

- 96 percent were overcoming space limitations (or were flexible about use of space and schedules)

- 91 percent were assertive about expanding their enrollment

- 85 percent provided personal evangelism training for the members

- 83 percent were assertive in creating and launching new classes

- 80 percent conducted organized weekly outreach

- 78 percent developed and maintained prospect lists

- 78 percent had high standards for leaders (either written commitments or signed covenants)

- 78 percent intentionally organized their classes with growth in mind (multiple leaders in classes and strong emphasis on age affinities)[4]

Why is it that some Sunday schools do not grow? Whatever the real answer, the fact is that many neglect to implement the principles that impact the potential growth. No key exists that will unlock the growth of the Sunday school. It is more like a combination lock and is more complex. Keep in mind that the fastest growing Sunday schools averaged nine of the

---

4. Ibid.

ten practices, and it was not the same nine for each church.[5] The work involved in implementing and sustaining multiple practices is a sacrifice that many pastors and leaders cannot or are not willing to make. The leadership of the Sunday school is often left to a sincere and well-meaning volunteer who primarily has responsibility for keeping records. To implement the ten practices described is a monumental task for a full-time staff member, let alone a volunteer. I fear that some leaders have abandoned Sunday school, not because it does not work but because of the work involved in making it work. They do not want to do what it will take to grow.

Dr. Thom Rainer came to a similar conclusion when studying the most effective evangelistic churches in North America: "Churches with ineffective Sunday schools violate the very principles that make Sunday school a viable organization: they dilute biblical teachings, fail to train effective teachers, replace systematic Bible teaching with other types of group activity, and relegate Sunday school to the status of one more church activity."[6] Every one of the ten practices is challenging to implement and to sustain month after month, and interestingly you will get resistance at each point. Many leaders will not want to participate in training. Some pastors do not want to be hands-on with the Sunday school. Some members will not want you to move their class. Many teachers will resist an open approach to enrollment. Some think that evangelism is the job of the staff. Many will not want you to "split" their class. Some teachers will not want to agree to a list of standards. It is interesting how universal the resistance is on the part of leaders in churches to the very practices that are common in churches with growing Sunday schools.

---

5. Ibid.
6. Rainer, *Effective Evangelistic Churches*, 82.

Serving as a pastor has enough challenges as it is without constantly dealing with these points of resistance. Sometimes it is easier to say that "it doesn't work" and focus on something else. It takes a lot of God's grace, a tremendous amount of patience, and the skillful guidance of a true leader to navigate a church into a position where they are utilizing the principles that can drive the growth of the Sunday school.

Is it possible for a Sunday school to experience growth in the general absence of the aforementioned practices? The answer is yes. Here are five other possibilities.

Seasonal Growth

Most Sunday schools will experience a mild surge of growth at two times during the year with little or no effort. The first is when school starts back in the late summer. Everyone is back in town from summer vacation and attendance can jump 10, 20, or 30 percent from the previous couple of months. Many churches also utilize this same time to reorganize classes, reenlist leaders, create new classes, and contact everyone about the changes. I call this the "Baptist New Year" in the churches where I serve. Likewise, a surge can occur in January in the actual New Year if the cold climate is not severe. Following a couple of weeks of school vacation and trips out of town to relatives, many people want to start the new year off right whether because of a resolution or a heartfelt conviction. Attendance can increase 10 to 20 percent compared with November and December. The seasonal growth is really an increase from the previous months and is not necessarily growth compared with the previous years. It can give an illusion of growth where it does not actually exist.

Population Growth

An influx of new neighborhoods can sometimes lead to growth in Sunday school with little effort. New families move into a new town, and many are believers who will be seeking a church for their families. The number of guests can increase, and a friendly congregation may see several new families join in a short span of time. The attendance can go up, and the members can boast of the growth in their church. All of this can happen without any lost or unchurched people being reached. A population surge will not, however, automatically equate with growth in attendance. Sometimes the wave of new members in the community brings in people of another race or culture than the congregation. Even if such newcomers are of the same faith, they are not always made to feel welcomed in the existing church. Sadly, some churches choose to die rather than receive (and be enriched by) other believers if they are not like those who established and led the church for many years. A church need not apologize for growing due to an increase in population, but we must not substitute the addition of Christian families from other communities for reaching out to the unchurched in the community.

Worship-Driven Growth

Some Sunday schools experience growth on the coat tails of the worship service. The worship service may be growing because of a primary focus on worship participation, a style of worship that appeals to the community, or a skilled staff member who provides key leadership in the worship. As the attendance at the worship service grows, the number of guests attending, the number of families joining, and hopefully the number of people trusting Christ increases. Some of the additional participants in the life of the church will find their way into the Sunday school. The rate of growth in the Sunday school will not equal that of the worship service in this scenario. The challenge is that those who are not connected to a small group generally do not find a place of service, tend not to provide strong financial support, and can inadvertently be overlooked when they have a crisis in their lives. The Sunday school in this situation can grow larger without growing stronger and ordinarily will not sustain the growth.

"New"-Driven Growth

When a church calls a new pastor or a new staff member or moves into a new facility, it will often experience a mild surge in growth that can include the Sunday school. The greatest potential of these is the call of a new pastor. It is not uncommon, though also not automatic, for attendance to flounder during an interim season without a pastor. Many members who have eased back on their attendance and perhaps some who may have been disgruntled begin to recommit and reestablish themselves when a new pastor is called. The appearance of growth may exist when compared with the previous months, but is not necessarily the result of the lost being reached.

Split-Driven Growth

I do not know how else to say it. A church down the road experiences a division causing many of the members to disperse into neighboring churches. It may or may not have been an actual "split" of the church. Nonetheless, five, ten, or even fifteen families immediately transfer to another church and quickly plug into the life of the new congregation, including the Sunday school. The church receiving the members can have the appearance of growth when none actually occurred (from a kingdom perspective). The decisions may be legitimate and the surge in attendance may be tangible, but the Sunday school may or may not be healthier when all is said and done.

A church or a staff member need not necessarily apologize if they have experienced growth for any of these reasons. In most instances the congregation should take advantage of the expanded base of leaders in order to minister more effectively and comprehensively. You should take time to ask where the growth is coming from. Do not allow the increase in average attendance to cause you to fall into a false sense of security that keeps you from implementing proven principle driven practices in the Sunday school, and more importantly in reaching out and bringing people into a personal relationship with Christ.

WHY SOME SUNDAY SCHOOLS DO NOT GROW

Some churches are located in sparsely populated areas that have very limited potential for growth. You would think that churches in communities with growing populations would all be thriving and that churches in rural areas would all be struggling. However, that is not the case. Churches can be found in both of these situations as well as everything in between that have Sunday schools that are growing and Sunday schools that are in decline. The Sunday schools that are in decline have the framework associated with a typical Sunday school strategy. They have the classrooms, the teachers, the curriculum, the furnishings, the schedule, and the general organization by age groupings that you will find in a growing Sunday school. However, the potential for growth has been sabotaged by one or more of the following demerits.

A Total Lack of Intention

The fact is that some leaders and some church members have no desire or intention to see growth in their church or their class. Their needs are being met, and that is all that matters. The lack of intention can also be the result of their perception of purpose. They believe that the purpose of the Sunday school is to teach the Bible. That can occur every week, and too often does, without any person ever being confronted with the gospel and brought to Christ. They may be blessed to experience a surge of growth for one of the aforementioned reasons but will never experience sustained growth in their ministry.

A Lack of Leadership

I have never seen a Sunday school experience long-term growth in the absence of leadership. Someone has to be out front leading the way. It begins with the pastor. If he does not emphasize Sunday school and elevate it, then growth will not happen. That is true of any area of ministry. In a smaller setting or in the initial stages of launching a Sunday school strategy, the pastor plays the role of a key leader. The point comes where others may be equipped to provide the hands-on leadership, and he shifts from being the key leader to the chief cheerleader. In any case, his leadership is always critical. Individual classes may grow in isolated situations because of the outstanding leadership of a teacher. On a churchwide scale, the pastor plays a critical role. The pastor's role is like that of a coach. The pastor is the leader of the organization, but he also stands on the sidelines and helps people to perform at their best. He sets direction and, to some degree, the game plan; but he does not do all of the work.[7] He must exercise his leadership through development and support of an equipping plan, as well as by publicly affirming his belief in the Sunday school strategy.

An Absence of Skills

Some pastors and teachers honestly want to see the Sunday school grow. They possess the "want to" but lack the "know how." Seminaries often fail to deliver the skills needed of the pastor in his early leadership development. The pastor assumes that Sunday school will work on autopilot, and when it does not, he does not know what to do. In some instances, he may have been told by a professor that the strategy cannot work. It is rare to find Sunday school leaders in a church who possess skills that

---

7. Allan Taylor, *The Six Core Values of Sunday School: A Philosophical, Practical, and Passionate Approach to Sunday School* (Canton, GA: Riverstone Group Publishing, 2003), 61.

the pastor does not have himself. How do you organize a class to be effective? How do you enlist leaders to help you in the process of accomplishing the purpose? How do you get members involved in outreach? How do you motivate people? How can you use enrollment as a tool for growth? How do you lead a class to release members to create a new class? The list goes on. The skills are not inherent and do not occur by osmosis. Someone has to teach them. The pastor or some key leader in the church must possess knowledge of those skills. In addition, the skills need to be taught to the Sunday school leaders.

Poorly Equipped Leaders

It is a sad fact that many people think Sunday school is boring because they had an experience with a boring Sunday school teacher. The reality is that it would continue to be boring by whatever name you assigned to it or whatever time the group gathered. The problem is not Sunday school as a strategy but a poorly equipped leader. The teacher is a volunteer and in his or her defense may not know any better. Teachers are often enlisted in churches and assigned to classes without any preparation or training. What gives some people the impression that the unchurched, immature believers, or students and young adults want to sleep in a Sunday school class that is not nearly as comfortable as their beds? Senior adults, because of their discipline, and younger children, because of having no choice in the matter, are often more tolerant of poor teaching. I am not suggesting that the aim of the Sunday school is to entertain. Sunday school teachers who are not equipped to prepare, teach with passion, utilize age-appropriate methods, and provide real-life application will inadvertently become a barrier to your Sunday school ministry.

An Assumption That Sunday School Is Outdated or Irrelevant

I have previously addressed the assumption that Sunday

school is outdated or irrelevant and need only make one additional point. This assumption is the equivalent of a football team going to play a game against an opponent they do not believe they can defeat. They have lost the game before the kickoff. Many Sunday schools are struggling because the pastor, staff, or other key leaders overtly or indirectly plant seeds of doubt in the minds of the congregation about the potential effectiveness of the Sunday school strategy.

MYTHS ABOUT SUNDAY SCHOOL GROWTH

In Baptist life we like to say that if you have four Baptists together, you have at least five or six opinions. I would imagine that tends to be true in your denomination or church also. In working with hundreds of pastors and thousands of Sunday school leaders, I have heard a ton of opinions on what will help the Sunday school to grow. Through my experience in leading Sunday schools to grow, I have found the following arguments to be of less consequence than many believe.

We would grow if we had better curriculum

The claim that better curriculum would result in growth is a myth I have heard stated by Sunday school teachers. I do not want to minimize the importance and the value of biblically based and relevant curriculum resources. They can certainly enhance the teaching and the learning experience. Keep in mind, however, that it is not good curriculum that makes the teaching good but good teaching that makes the curriculum good. You can give the best curriculum available to an unskilled teacher and he or she will not be able to use it effectively. At the same time you can give a skilled teacher a basic outline with a couple of ideas and he or she will make it come to life. Curriculum choices are important, and the church should give it due attention. However, it is the skill of the teacher in communicating God's Word rather than the specific teaching resources that has the most impact on the growth of the class.

We would grow if we had more staff

Some say more staff will cause growth, yet it is a myth. Perhaps it should be true to say we would grow if we had more staff, but it is not always the case. I can point to churches with no full-time staff that are growing and multistaffed churches that are not growing. If you are waiting on more staff to see your Sunday school or your Sunday school class grow, you have lost focus. Within a class a teacher will likewise say that the class would grow if there were more leaders. You may be right, but while you are waiting on more leaders to join or be sent to your class, you are missing a lot of opportunities. One leader can make a difference. You are that leader! Exercise the leadership that God has called you to provide, and don't be surprised when He sends others to help you.

We would grow if we were more innovative

The myth that innovation produces growth reflects the fascination of our culture with all things new. A Sunday school that is struggling will have to make some adjustments if the desire is to be healthy and growing. Some may be inclined to believe that the key to success is creativity or adopting a new "cutting edge" approach. Exercising creativity and having an awareness of the newest in trends is of value. However, it may or may not be the solution for your class or church. The aim should be effectiveness in accomplishing the purpose of the Sunday school. You may be led to believe in some of the materials that you read that established churches are all in decline and that the innovative churches are all flourishing. That is not the case. Do not hesitate to be innovative, but do not think that innovation is a magic bullet that will turn your Sunday school around.

We would grow if we were located somewhere else

Another myth is the notion that location alone produces growth. Location does have an effect on the potential growth and size of a congregation because of population variations. I have been amazed, however, where I have found growing Sunday schools in our state. I know of a church located seventeen miles from the nearest high school that has flourished for the last decade. This example is not an isolated case. I visit churches like this one every month. I live in a community that has grown by more than 500 percent over the past twenty years. Yet there are congregations within a few miles of my community that have the same average attendance that they had before the population surge occurred (and it is not because they are releasing members to plant churches). The size of the congregation may be limited by the location, but growth can occur wherever unchurched people live. Most every community in the United States is 60 to 90 percent unchurched (depending on where you live). Do the math. Statistically, a community with a population of only 1,500 has at least 900 people who are unchurched. Growth requires the presence of the unchurched, and they are the majority of most any community.

We would grow if we had more resources

The myth that having more resources generates growth is another common perspective. Resources are usually thought of in terms of finances and facilities. You need not apologize for desiring these resources and for making efforts to secure them. Many churches have a "field of dreams" vision of growth: "If we build it, they will come." Here again, there are plenty of churches that have finances and facilities yet are not growing, and churches meeting in rented or borrowed spaces that are reaching the unchurched. The greatest resource is the Holy Spirit, and the greatest tools are committed leaders. Do not be lulled into missing ministry opportunities while waiting on resources to arrive. They are advantageous, but not always essential.

Do you want your class and your church to grow? I believe that God does. The reason is that kingdom growth is ultimately the result of people trusting Christ as Savior. I have no doubt that God is in favor of that result. Many congregations do not want their church to grow. They do not want the church to get "big." If your members have this attitude, growth is not likely to be an issue because growth is highly unlikely. Are you going to turn away those whom God wants to save and to grow because you do not want your church to get "big"? Whose church is it anyway? Remember that the church belongs to Christ. He has commissioned the church to "go and make disciples." The real question is, do you want to be obedient? If so, you will find your class and your congregation being intentional in partnering with God as instruments so that the lost are reached, lives are changed, and leaders are sent. Keep in mind that you have an alternative that will allow you to be in a church that grows by reaching the lost while remaining at a size that is preferable to the existing congregation. The solution is to purposefully release members as you grow to plant new churches or to go as missionaries to help struggling congregations. After all, a Sunday school that really works is one where "leaders are sent."

How do you get the "want to" into your congregation or your class? Some of these actions are detailed in other parts of this work. However, here is a summary and some words of challenge. First, you must pray. "And when they had prayed, the place where they were assembled together was shaken; and they were all filled with the Holy Spirit, and they spoke the word of God with boldness" (Acts 4:31). That is what needs to happen to your Sunday school and to your members. It was the result of prayer. God must touch the hearts of your members and place in them a desire to grow as a result of touching lives in your community.

Secondly, you must take responsibility. Pray for yourself as you pray for others. Do you really want to see your Sunday school grow? If so, you must be willing to make sacrifices of time and energy to be used of God in leading your church or class to reach out beyond your walls.

Thirdly, you must learn the skills and dynamics that are critical to the leadership of a Sunday school ministry or class. Your time invested in reading this book is a good step. Once you finish you must continue the journey by applying what you have learned and seeking other opportunities to grow in your knowledge and skills.

Finally, you must make training a priority. Leaders cannot apply what they do not know. They do not know what they have not been taught. People are easily distracted. Life is filled with responsibilities and challenges that cry out for our attention each and every day. You must persistently draw the attention of leaders back to the principles and practices that enhance the environment for growth by providing and participating in training opportunities on a regular basis. The "want to" comes easier when people understand "why" and "how." Do you want your Sunday school to grow? Read on!

DISCUSSION QUESTIONS

1. Review the ten practices of the fastest growing Sunday schools. Evaluate and discuss the practices of your ministry in comparison to these practices.

2. How would you characterize the "want to" of your congregation and the leadership of the church? What are the barriers that prevent some of your congregation and leaders from wanting to grow?

3. What steps can you take to affect the passion of your congregation for reaching the unchurched and growing the Sunday school ministry?

CHAPTER 5

A Sunday School That Really WORKS . . .

Organizes to Grow

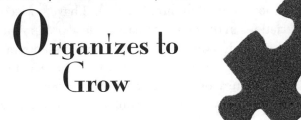

WHAT IS IT GOING TO TAKE?

Leading a Sunday school or a class to grow begins with desire, but it does not end there. Some leaders are under the impression that if they work harder, the Sunday school will grow. That is not necessarily true. If your car is out of gas, you can work as hard as you want on the transmission and you still will not get power until you put gas in the tank. Working hard is important, but working at the right things is more important. Perhaps you think your Sunday school would grow if people just loved Jesus more. I would not argue that every congregation needs to love Jesus more, but I believe that by and large the leaders I work with really do love the Lord. What they often lack is the know-how or the skill. Others might suggest that the Sunday school would grow if we would "just teach the Bible." The Bible should be taught with authority and with passion, which is already happening in many Sunday schools that are not growing. Teaching sound doctrine cannot be neglected but also cannot be assumed to automatically lead to growth.

I have observed and studied growing Sunday schools for many years. I have found in the growing and the nongrowing churches that the people love God, that they love the Word of God, that they pray, that they love one another, and that they love their church. Yes, there are exceptions, but these characteristics are present more often than not. However, I have noticed that there are variations in the characteristics of leadership. The issues that we are about to consider have been addressed strategically and purposefully in some cases and in others have just become a part of the culture of the congregation over the course of time. I believe that being purposeful about an issue is the way that the church culture is influenced. Consider the following four leadership issues and contrast them with your church.

The pastor elevates the Sunday school

What happens when a pastor never mentions or promotes missions? The congregation tends to neglect to give to or participate in missions opportunities. What happens when a pastor neglects to emphasize evangelism? The congregation tends to ignore the lost and to become inwardly focused. Over the course of time, the congregation tends to prioritize whatever it is that the pastor elevates. You will not likely find a church where the pastor de-emphasizes or neglects Sunday school as a priority on the one hand and yet leads the Sunday school to grow on the other.

I want to acknowledge from personal experience that pastors already have full plates. I want to share two points of encouragement along this line. First, elevating the Sunday school does not require dozens of more hours on your part each week. I am not saying that it does not take time, but it may be more attainable than you realize. Second, consider the benefits gained by a growing Sunday school. As the Sunday school grows, the leadership base grows, the financial base grows, the worship service grows, the number of people trusting Christ as Savior grows, the music ministry grows, and the student ministry grows. It does not end there. Where else could you invest your time that would provide your congregation with this extent of results?

What is the pastor's role? In the early stages of launching growth or in the circumstance that leaders are lacking, the pastor serves as the key leader of the Sunday school, meaning that you may need to serve as the Sunday school director for a year or two. You may have to temporarily adjust personal priorities until other leaders are trained. You need to develop knowledge of the growth principles and lead the congregation to apply them. You may not have learned them in seminary and may need to read other materials in addition to these. (For some suggestions, see the bibliography following the appendixes.)

It will likely take a hands-on approach by the pastor to get the momentum going. Once you gain momentum, the role of the pastor transitions from key leader to chief cheerleader. It is at this point that others provide the hands-on leadership and you provide encouragement, verbal affirmation, counsel, and expertise as you continue to cast vision. Here are ten ways that a pastor can elevate the Sunday school:

1. *Publicly declare to your congregation your conviction about the importance of Sunday school.* Have they heard this from you before? Do not assume that they know.

2. *Give a brief weekly Sunday school report each week prior to worship if it fits the flow of your service.* You affirm and praise when attendance is up. You challenge and invite when attendance is down. You should never complain to those present about those who are absent.

3. *Have a commissioning service for your Sunday school leaders each year.* This service will permit you to affirm

your Sunday school leaders while promoting the Sunday school ministry. This is best done at the beginning of the Sunday school year.

4. *Incorporate Sunday school testimonies into your worship service.* You could do this for several consecutive Sundays or spread them throughout the year. Allow your congregation to hear how classes have ministered to one another in times of need, how people have been reached, and how lives have been affected.

5. *Regularly write about Sunday school in your newsletters or bulletins.* Take the opportunity a couple of times a year to elevate and affirm the value of Sunday school through your written communication.

6. *Personally enlist, train, and meet regularly with your Sunday school director.* This is one leadership position that should not be left to a nominating team and cannot be neglected if growth is the aim. Meet with your director at least monthly to debrief and strategize together.

7. *Develop a Sunday school planning team.* The team should consist of the pastor, Sunday school director, age-group staff members, and a teacher from each of the four age groups (preschoolers, children, students, and adults). Meet three to four times a year to strategize.

8. *Preach occasionally on Sunday school themes.* You can develop messages or incorporate points that emphasize the importance and value of participation in a small group.

9. *Seek ways to increase your personal expertise.* Your

members will not know nor grasp the principles of growth if you do not understand them!

10. *Make Sunday school leader training a priority in your church.* Your leaders will not apply the principles unless they are taught and continually refreshed.

In his research for *Effective Evangelistic Churches,* Thom Rainer observed that "effective Sunday schools had strong and vocal support from the pastor. Indeed, it was often the pastor who spoke most often about the importance of Sunday school. He did not leave the emphasis in the hands of a minister of education or a Sunday school director alone. The pastor typically was actively involved in training, recruiting, and promotion in Sunday School."[1] Similarly, Ken Hemphill in *Revitalizing the Sunday Morning Dinosaur* provides the following insight into the pastor's role:

> Some pastors consider Sunday school the domain of professional educators. Pastors often receive little seminary training about the work of the Sunday school, and they do not feel prepared to lead the Sunday school. Many have dreamed of the day that they could afford to employ a professional educator to lead the Sunday school. But many pastors will never lead a multiple-staff church. Most churches are single-staff churches. Thus if the Sunday school program is to work effectively, the pastor must assume leadership. Yet even in the larger churches with specialized educational staffs, the Sunday school will not function as a powerful growth tool if the pastor does not provide leadership. The people will usually make the greatest commitment to that which the pastor gives greatest emphasis. Laypersons commit to serve

---

1. Rainer, *Effective Evangelistic Churches,* 172.

in the Sunday school when they see that this is their pastor's priority.[2]

You will find that churches with growing Sunday schools have pastors who have discovered the way of elevating the Sunday school and the importance of doing so.

The Sunday school leaders are purposefully equipped

Did you know that the impact of training on Sunday school leaders is quantifiable? The Georgia Baptist Convention surveys member churches annually to identify patterns and to learn from the churches. A question was included in a recent annual church profile regarding the training patterns of the churches. The churches were asked if they met with their Sunday school leaders weekly, monthly, quarterly, annually, randomly (other), or never. The question revealed that 40 percent of the churches did not provide any training for their leaders in the previous twelve months. The growth patterns of the church were distinctly varied between the churches that provided training and those that did not. Once the training patterns were identified the churches were grouped based on frequency of training.[3]

The churches reporting that they had provided quarterly training had grown 13.8 percent in the past three years (when all averaged together). The churches that provided monthly training grew 13.4 percent in the same time frame. Only eighty-eight churches reported that they met weekly with their leaders. They had grown 6.5 percent. This does not suggest that weekly training is less effective but more likely reflects that churches conducting weekly training tend to be larger. A similar net gain in a larger Sunday school would be a smaller percentage gain than a smaller church. The churches that met

---

2. Hemphill, *Revitalizing the Sunday Morning Dinosaur*, 21.
3. See table 3.1. on page 63.

annually had grown 4.2 percent and those who responded that they meet randomly (or other) had grown 0.8 percent. Only one group remains. What happened in the churches that did not meet with their leaders last year? Their cumulative growth was negative 2.1 percent. They are the churches that tend to be in decline—40 percent of the churches surveyed.

It is not a coincidence that the Sunday schools in these (nonequipping) churches are declining. The health and growth of the Sunday school requires that leadership training opportunities are provided and likewise that the Sunday school teachers and their leaders participate in those opportunities.

Expectations are established and communicated

The apostle Paul wrote out expectations for deacons and pastors in 1 Timothy 3 and Titus 1. He proposed that there were minimum standards of conduct and character that should be expected of key church leaders. The office of the small group leader or the Sunday school teacher was not part of the church landscape at that point in history. However, the principle of standards for key church leaders was established and still applies today.

Which of the following scenarios is most likely to provide the best quality of leadership and the best results? In the first instance, a nominating committee enlists a teacher to lead a class and provides the teacher with the date, place, and class with little or no additional orientation or training. In the second instance, a leader directly enlists a teacher to serve under his or her leadership providing a basic list of expectations including a commitment to participate in an orientation session and regular training throughout the year. Assuming that both prospective teachers accept the invitation, who do you suppose will be most effective? You may think that it is harder to enlist a leader if you establish expectations. In the short term it can be difficult, but in the long term the culture of the church adjusts to having such expectations and the results are greater.

Having expectations of Sunday school leaders is "no big deal" in churches that have been doing so over a period of time.

How do you introduce and implement expectations if teachers have been enlisted without written standards in the past? Begin by enlisting a team to develop written ministry descriptions for key Sunday school leaders. Be sure to include training expectations in the descriptions, but do not construct a list containing too many points. Identify minimal expectations with a list of five or six points at the most. These can be expanded in later years as expectations are raised. Once completed, present these to the leaders as *general guidelines*. The leaders do not need to sign these at this point. Give these to leaders upon enlistment the next time your Sunday school year begins. Transition the heading for the *general guidelines* to *leadership commitments* the following year. The leaders make a verbal commitment to serve by these standards as they are enlisted. In later years you may choose to transition from *leadership commitment* to *leadership covenants* that leaders sign to indicate their commitment to serve by the written standards. At that point the leaders are absolutely committed to participate in the equipping plan as proposed in the covenant.

The level of comfort varies from church to church in relation to how far to go in implementing commitments and covenants. However, having no written guidelines or descriptions is a recipe for low expectations and low results. Implement the *general guidelines* at a minimum. You will find the list that I use as a starting point for churches in appendixes C and D.

Implementing expectations is a challenge. Thom Rainer made the following observation about high expectations in his nationwide study of effective churches:

> In our interviews with the leaders of the higher-assimilation churches, we asked if their moving of Sunday schools to become high-expectation organizations had caused any

problems. Their answers were an unequivocal "yes." Some teachers and leaders refused to agree to stricter require-ments and dropped out of ministry and service. Others resisted, implying that high-expectations in Sunday school hinted of legalism.

Never did we hear that the expectation issue was ad-dressed with ease. But in virtually every case, the pastor or staff member told us that the pain was worth the gains realized.[4]

There are two more notes that I want to place on the table at this point. The first is to those of you who are Sunday school teachers. Please do not resist the implementation of standards when suggested by your leaders. It is not an insult to you but an effort to ensure better quality of leadership in the future. It is certainly acceptable to work with your leaders to deter-mine reasonable standards, but to suggest that there should be none is a detriment to the church and ministry that you love. The other note is to pastors and leaders. Seek God's wisdom in the pace of implementation. You will have a catastrophe if you try to move from no expectations to signed covenants in thirty days. Take it one step at a time. Move forward, but do not move too fast.

The Sunday school teachers are committed to be Sunday school leaders

Take a couple of minutes to think about the following state-ment: A Sunday school teacher can potentially have an impact on a class. In actuality, a Sunday school leader will always have an impact on a class. Teaching may or may not result in learning and life change. However, leadership by definition re-quires a response by the follower. Otherwise, no leadership has

---

4. Rainer, *High Expectations*, 35.

taken place. Teachers by the thousands teach Sunday school lessons each and every week. The sad fact is that many class members are unmoved and have no concern for the exercise of their spiritual gifts or the evangelism of the lost. You can teach your class without ever leading. To lead your class will always require that you do a good job of teaching. Your class members are busy going about their lives and are daily pulled in many directions. They want someone who will help them to refocus on a regular basis and will motivate them to serve God. Are you teaching or are you leading?

HELP! I'M TOO BUSY TO ORGANIZE!

I hope you are convinced that a healthy Sunday school class is one where the lost are being reached, lives are being changed, and leaders are being sent. That may sound good on paper, but you may face a common dilemma. You are a busy person. I know that because Sunday school leaders are some of the busiest people in the church. Not only do you lead a Sunday school class, but you also sing in the choir or on the praise team, serve on more than one leadership team or committee, and on top of that coach a little league team. Of course, that is in addition to being a full-time mom, owning your own business, or working fifty to sixty hours each week. You do well to prepare a Sunday school lesson and deliver it on Sunday. How could anyone expect you to lead your class to reach out to the unchurched and to grow? It takes a lot of work to position your class so that God can bring the results that you desire. That is why a Sunday school that works organizes to grow.

You cannot do it on your own. Moses could not lead the people on his own. Nehemiah could not rebuild the walls of Jerusalem on his own. Gideon could not defeat the enemy on his own. The New Testament pastors could not lead the early church on their own, and they purposefully enlisted Spirit-filled men (deacons) to assist with the ministry tasks. If these heroes of the faith needed help from above and help from their peers, then what about you? I am not suggesting that you need to organize for the sake of organization or because you read it in a book. You need to organize so that God can maximize the potential for the ministry to which He has called you. Add to these challenges the fact that you may not possess administrative gifts. What are you going to do? You can teach each week with occasional experiences of blessing. Or you can determine that you will invest time in organization in order to maximize your potential. Why go at it alone when God has given you a team? You need to learn how to organize the team to accomplish all that God intends.

Effective organization is not an add-on to your responsibility but rather a common practice found in the most effective evangelistic churches. Here is how Thom Rainer summarized what he discovered about organization in North America's most effective churches: "In the higher-assimilation churches, basic organizational principles were at work continuously. Teachers were trained and taught weekly. New members were assigned to classes. Care groups were created in all classes so that ministry could be effective. Outreach and evangelism were organized through the Sunday school."[5] Likewise, we discovered in a study of the fastest growing Sunday schools in Georgia that one of the common practices was that they were intentional in organizing their Sunday school classes for growth.

Organizing the Sunday school to grow is done on two levels. You must determine how to organize from a congregational perspective and then assist leaders with organizing the individual classes or groups. Most churches have a structure in place for organizing the congregation but neglect to equip leaders on the organization of the individual units. Don't get sidetracked by terminology as you consider organizational strategies. Focus

---

5. Ibid., 37.

on the principles and purposes behind the terms. The terms may vary from church to church. Consider these issues in the following questions when evaluating whether or not your congregation has a Sunday school organized to grow.

Do you have classes for all age groups?

The smallest of congregations will need a minimum of four classes. You need at least one class for preschoolers (birth through kindergarten), one for children (grades one through six), one for students (grades seven through twelve), and one for adults (high school graduates and older). Each of these classes will eventually become departments or divisions as classes are added. You may think that you do not need a preschool class because your church is small and you do not have any preschoolers. The reality is that you do not have any preschool age children because you do not have a class for them.

Do you have enough classes?

A large class can provide lots of enthusiasm. However, you do not want a class with twenty-five two-year-olds! You may be able to get by with an adult class that has twenty-five in attendance. Yet you still must consider if the teacher will be able to provide ministry to all of those adults in addition to as many as twenty-five others who are members of the class but do not attend regularly. The class sizes need to be large enough to have good interaction, discussion, and fellowship while being small enough for the teacher to provide ministry to each member. Larger churches will tend to have larger classes. You need approximately one class for every ten attending or every twenty enrolled with a minimum of four classes (one for each age group). You can have a slightly higher ratio, but bear in mind that the further you stray from my suggested guideline, the more difficult it will be for your volunteer teachers to maintain contact and ministry to all of the members and the potential growth is then affected.

Do you have enough leaders for the existing classes?

The number of leaders will vary by age group. The younger the audience, the smaller the ratio of leaders to learners needs to be. For example, you need one adult for every two babies that are present but will only need one adult for as many as ten high school age students. However, there are some minimums that you need to apply. Each preschool, children's, and student class should have at least two unrelated adults in each class. The liability insurance held by your church compels this from a legal perspective, and it makes good sense from a practical perspective. It is a way to protect children, provide for accountability, and spread responsibility beyond one adult leader. Adult classes need only one teacher, but that teacher needs to involve as many adults as possible in leadership through the use of their spiritual gifts. Further instruction on leadership enlistment and organization of adult classes will be covered as we move forward.

Are you organized to maximize spiritual growth?

All of the members will gather together for the worship service. However, the small groups are broken down by age groupings that allow you to target various stages of intellectual and social development. You cannot maximize the growth of a seventeen-year-old girl by having her on the level of a third-grade boy. They need to be in different groups to focus on their needs and abilities based on their life stage. The groupings can be organized to enhance the ability of participants to grow spiritually as leaders are enlisted and new classes are created. Plan to add more preschool, children, student, and adult classes with the goal of narrowing the difference in maturity levels as you organize to grow. Organize your preschool classes by age with the intent of avoiding age spans greater than three years and aiming for spans of two years or less. A bed baby and a kindergarten preschooler are worlds apart in their spiritual and physical development. Both need care and instruction from loving adults. Organize children and student classes by grade. Avoid grade spans greater than three years when possible and aim for spans of only two years as you add classes. In addition, older children and younger youth will often flourish more in a gender-based group rather than a coed grouping. Organize adults by life stage or age. Avoid age spans of more than fifteen years and aim for spans of ten years or less as you add classes.

Are you organized based on who attends or who you desire to reach?

You will find it difficult to experience sustained growth if you organize based on those who are attending. The adult ministry is primarily where this becomes an issue. Many Sunday schools have a Young Couples Class that has members in their forties. You are unlikely to reach new young couples if that is the case. You need to start a new Young Couples Class every three to five years. The worship service is an intergenerational experience. The adult Sunday school functions best at reaching and assimilating new people when organized by life stage or more narrow age groupings. Do not be afraid of assigning an age grouping to each adult class. Remember that a class name does not communicate who the class is intended for. Include age targets with class names or name classes by life stage such as Parent of Preschoolers, College and New Career, Nearly and Newlyweds, etc. Your members may think that it makes sense for everyone to go where they are comfortable. The reality is that a commitment to reach the lost and to connect them to the congregation requires that we organize in a way that assists in reaching and assimilating them. Here is a step-by-step process for organizing or reorganizing the adult Sunday school to reach new people:

1. Conduct a survey of adult classes to determine the age of each person attending each class.

2. Identify the core grouping of each class and identify absence of any age groupings in attendance.

3. Designate all existing classes with an age target based on core groupings.

4. Change the signs on doors and in promotion to identify who attends that class or group based on age grouping or life stage.

5. Communicate that the groupings are not absolute. The designated age groupings represent the target.

6. Assign future prospects and members to the appropriate grouping.

7. Create new classes to account for any gaps to ensure that a place is provided for all ages and life stages.

8. Have an annual Realignment Sunday to evaluate, reorganize, reassign space, and create new classes.

9. Use class names internally for class unity and spirit.

You will face several organizational challenges as a Sunday school leader. How do you organize your class/group for maximum effectiveness? Where do you find the leaders you need to help you? How do you motivate people to get involved? Let us consider how you might more effectively tackle these common organizational challenges.

ORGANIZING CLASSES FOR MAXIMUM EFFECTIVENESS

Should you have a traditional or an innovative structure? That is the wrong question. The aim is to be effective, and you will find churches that are doing well with a variety of structures. What they have in common is that they intentionally organize and engage their members in the exercise of their gifts. Purposeful organization is a principle that can take several forms (methods) and still be effective. Therefore, do not get bogged down with terminology. Should you have a Sunday school superintendent, Sunday school director, or small group coach? If it is the wrong person for the role, it will not matter what the title is. If it is the right person, it will not matter either. He or she will get the job done. Should you have an outreach director, outreach coordinator, visitation leader, or a marketplace evangelism team leader? Again, the title is not as important as the leader and the assignment that person is given. Use the terminology that fits into your context and move forward. That being said, look beyond any titles that I am about to propose and focus on the organizational principles at work.

You may be surprised to learn that not every class or group should be organized in the same way. The way you organize a class or group that averages four in attendance and a class or group that averages twenty-four in attendance will not be the same. The way that you organize a senior adult class and a preschool class will not be the same. You do not need to organize your class based on a chart, and therefore I am not going to provide you with one. But you should organize based on key principles. Consider the following class organizational principles and the questions included and organize your class based on the principles. If you apply the principles you may find yourself leading a Sunday school class that really works.

The Principle of Two: You do not have an organization if you are leading the class by yourself

Any class, no matter how large or how small and no matter what age grouping, needs a minimum of two leaders. In addition, you must consider security and liability issues if you teach a class that involves students or children less than eighteen years of age. Any preschool, children's, or student class must have a minimum of two unrelated adults present at all times to minimize liability issues as well as to maximize educational effectiveness. Perhaps you teach an adult class. You need at least one person to assist with record keeping and other tasks that you cannot attend to while fulfilling your teaching responsibilities. In addition, you need someone to assist you in accomplishing the aims of the class and to compensate for any shortcomings you may have with time, experience, giftedness, or energy. You must remember that where you are weak there are others who are strong. You need someone else to work with you to lead the class. How should responsibility be divided between the two of you? A healthy class is one where the lost are being reached, lives are being changed, and leaders are being sent. Therefore, be intentional in enlisting others to assist you in accomplishing these aims.

The Principle of Targets: If you aim at nothing, you will hit it every time

You have two broad targets that you need to aim at as a class. The first is the *target of purpose* and the second is the *target of need*. Remember that the purpose of Sunday school is to enable the church to strategically embrace and engage the Great Commission. Your class will be accomplishing that purpose when the lost are being reached, lives are being changed, and leaders are being sent. You need to organize your class to fulfill the purpose more than to fill in an organizational chart. You should resolve to take responsibility to teach and lead in such a way that "lives will be changed" as you faithfully prepare and present God's Word each week. You should follow that resolve by enlisting and cooperating with another leader to develop strategies that will help you lead the class to reach out to the lost. Most groups would refer to this position as an outreach leader, and that is sufficient, but what is most important is that you enlist another leader to assist you in fulfilling that particular purpose.

Although this task is integral to the Great Commission and to the historical and biblical purpose of the Sunday school, it is perhaps the most neglected. The key is not to delegate the task but to enlist someone to partner with you to accomplish the aim of keeping the members focused on this component of the class purpose. The other component is that "leaders are being sent." Leaders cannot be sent unless they are first developed in your class. You and your partner can begin the process of preparing leaders by giving attention to the second target, which is the "target of need."

What does your class need in order to be effective? I would encourage you to make a list (or work with your class to do so) and to place the needs in priority order. You have a tremendous advantage if you lead an adult class. A preschool class may have to rely on only two adult leaders to meet all of the needs of their class. However, an adult class can and should get others involved.

Once you have your list prioritized, begin to enlist individuals or teams to take responsibility for leading the class to meet that need. If you identify prayer as a need, enlist a prayer leader or a prayer team. If you identify fellowship as a need, enlist a fellowship leader or a fellowship team. If you identify ministry as a need, enlist a ministry leader or a ministry team. Prioritizing is critical at this point. If you lead a smaller class you may be able to find leaders to address only one or two of the needs. Start with the needs based on the priorities, but seek to discover and engage that third leader as soon as possible. Dozens of possibilities and dozens of ways to organize are available. The key is to get your class focused on the right targets and to enlist leaders who will aim your class at the targets.

The Principle of Teams: Every leader has limitations of time and energy

The most dynamic Sunday school teacher still has only twenty-four hours for each day and can be only one place at a time. It is not possible for the teacher to do all of the work alone and accomplish the mission and aims of the class. *The more people you enlist to help you with the class, the more people the class will reach and, ultimately, the more leaders your class will send to serve others.* Every believer in your group has been gifted by the Holy Spirit to serve the body. Your function as the teacher is to lead them to exercise their gifts. When that is done, it benefits you as the teacher, it benefits the class, but most importantly, it benefits the body of Christ.

It is not a complicated principle. Think about it. Which class will accomplish the most? Would it be the class where the teacher provides all of the leadership or the class where the teacher involves six other members in working together to provide the leadership? Once you determine and prioritize needs, begin enlisting leaders and teams to take responsibility.

Perhaps you want more specific direction for organizing your group. I am going to provide you with a list of common leadership roles that classes and Bible study groups need. Remember not to get hung up on the titles that I use. In addition, keep in mind that the list is not exhaustive but is intended to assist you if you need more specific guidance. Enlist leaders in the following order of priority:

1. Teacher/Group Leader

2. Secretary/Class Administrator or Coordinator

3. Prayer Leader (who may enlist a prayer team)

4. Outreach Leader (and Prayer Leader in small class)

5. Care Group Coordinator (who should enlist Care Group Leaders to maintain contact with members)

6. Fellowship Coordinator (can be combined with Outreach Leader in a smaller class)

In addition, a larger class can determine other needs and enlarge the leadership base. You would also do well to place all regular participants on a team with one of these leaders. What would happen if you had seven, eight, or nine others providing leadership? That is the key. But the question is, how do you get the class members to help?

WHERE DO I FIND THE LEADERS TO HELP?

A young man courageously asks out a beautiful co-worker for a dinner date one weekend. She rejects the invitation without hesitation. He makes the mistake of asking a follow-up question. "Why not?" he asks. "Is there someone else?" She replies, "There's got to be!" You may be struggling to find the help that you need to lead your class. Is there something that you can do that will make a difference? "There's got to be," and there is! The short answer to the question is that they are right in front of you. The question comes down to how do you get them engaged in service?

You need to keep a couple of things in mind if you are the teacher or the group leader. First of all, leading your class members to serve is the reason that God has placed you in the group. You may be thinking, *No, I am here to teach them God's Word.* Jesus commanded in the Great Commission that we are to teach them to obey all that He has commanded us. Does that not require you to teach your members to serve? Furthermore, the Bible states that we are to be "doers of the word and not hearers only" (James 1:22). What is the value of your teaching if your class members are not engaged in service either inside or outside of the group? A lack of response by your group members does not mean that you should quit but that you should commit. Secondly, a Great Commission class is one where "leaders are being sent." How can you ultimately send leaders to serve outside of your group if they are unwilling to serve inside of your group? I propose that you will rarely be able to. As you enlist them to serve and help them to exercise their gifts, God uses them to strengthen your class and will often urge them toward even greater levels of commitment and service. Consider the following ideas and principles for the discovery and enlistment of leaders.

HOW TO FIND AND ENLIST LEADERS

First, the most common method of enlistment is also the least effective. Suppose you determine that you need an outreach leader. The most typical approach to enlistment is to stand before your class and include an appeal during the time of announcements: "The pastor says that we all need to have an outreach leader. Let me know if you are interested." Following this bold proclamation, people are lined up to see you after your Bible study class to beg for the privilege of being named to the new leadership position. Is that the way it happens in your church? I didn't think so. You have committed no sin by announcing the need for an outreach leader, and you may be blessed occasionally to enlist someone in that manner. However, this approach rarely works and the leader often walks away frustrated at the "lack of commitment of the class members." Feel free to use this approach, but do not anticipate a lot of results.

Second, begin with the strategy that Jesus modeled. Do you recall Matthew 9:37-38? "Then He said to His disciples, 'The harvest truly is plentiful, but the laborers are few. Therefore pray the Lord of the harvest to send out laborers into His harvest.'" You may recall that Jesus prayed all night before approaching the men that he would call (enlist) to be His apostles. Are you praying for God to raise up and call out leaders within your class? Are you really? Begin praying yourself and then engage your class in praying for God to raise up leaders from your class and for your class. Pray fervently and regularly. Be prepared for God to call some members out of your class also. As you pray with your class you will have opportunity to lead them to pray about their place of service within the class. Ask them to share with you personally what God is saying to them through the times of prayer about their role within the class. Feel free to remind them that attendance is appreciated but that it does not equate with service or leadership.

Third, commit to your personal growth as a leader. People follow leaders. Spiritual leadership begins with spiritual growth. Examine yourself spiritually and prioritize your personal relationship with God. Some things in life are better caught than taught. How is your level of passion? How is your relationship with the Lord? Remember that people are attracted to leaders who are authentic and have a passion for what they do. Are you excited about what God is doing in your life and in your ministry? If not, then why should anyone else be, and why would they want to serve alongside you? Do not stop with your spiritual growth. Are you developing as a leader? The fact that you are reading this book is a good indication that you are. What comes next? What are you going to do to sharpen your skills as a leader? Leaders tend to attract other leaders. You must grow, and as you do you will find it easier (though not necessarily easy) to enlist leaders.

Fourth, you need to take the time to purposefully and directly enlist leaders to serve. Why can't you save time by making a general announcement to the class? It is because they all think you are talking about someone else. You need to know something about the members of your class that attend regularly. They really do love and appreciate you. That is why they are there every week in your class or group. They would do almost anything you ask them to do if it was in their power. If you called them now because you were having car trouble, they would do all in their power to help out. When you announce that you need an outreach leader, they do not think you are talking about them but rather someone else.

How was it that Jesus enlisted the apostles? Did he make a public announcement and ask them to sign up if interested? No. According to Luke 6, he prayed all night. As you study the New Testament account you will discover that He went and directly invited them to follow Him. Begin by praying about who should be the outreach leader for your class. Ask God to show you. Once He does, you need to ask to meet with that person privately (not beside the welcome center in the hallway) or with you and your spouse or another member if the person is of the opposite sex. Tell the individual that God has placed something on your heart that you want to share. When you meet, you should share what you have been praying about and what God has placed on your heart. Share two or three things that you expect of an outreach leader (or whatever the role) and how long the commitment will be. You do not want an immediate answer; ask the individual to pray about helping in this area, and indicate that you will check back in a few days.

You will get one of three responses from the people you ask: (1) The individual will likely say yes, and you will have your leader. (2) The individual may say no, and you must trust that God will deal with the disobedience or that He is leading in some other way. You have complimented the individual by asking and God may be purposefully using your encouragement. (3) The individual may respond that he or she is not comfortable with outreach but wonder if there is some other way to help. That would be a blessing. The person might not have served at all had you not suggested the role of outreach leader. Enlisting directly in this manner is more time consuming. However, you will get better results because it is based in prayer and engages the Holy Spirit in the enlistment process.

Fifth, enlistment is a task that you must attend to throughout the year. Enlistment is not something you do only at the beginning of the year. Look for leaders continually. Expand the leadership base month by month as you have more time to enlist additional leaders. You will be amazed at how much more your class or group can do, how much it frees you up to focus on your strengths, and how God uses it to send leaders from your class to help in other critical areas such as preschool, children, students, and in the creation of new classes. Remember that all preschool, children, and youth teachers come from adult classes. Enlist leaders, engage them in service, and extend the influence of your ministry by releasing some members every year to serve in other areas of importance. Yours can truly be a class where the lost are reached, lives are changed, and leaders are sent.

HOW DO I MOTIVATE PEOPLE TO PARTICIPATE AND LEAD?

Everyone needs an occasional nudge from someone else to help him or her focus or get involved in a greater way. That nudge is what your class or group members are looking for from you. You are their leader. They look to you for inspiration as well as biblical instruction. What can be done to motivate your members? Begin by asking yourself what other leaders do to motivate you. Think about that for a few moments. Make a list and practice those things yourself. Perhaps your list includes some of the following.

Prayer

"And when they had prayed, the place where they were assembled together was shaken; and they were all filled with the Holy Spirit and they spoke the word of God with boldness" (Acts 4:31). The Holy Spirit of God is the greatest motivator. How can God indwell a person with the power of His Spirit and not have an impact on his or her life? Pray for your class and group members by name and ask God to work mightily in their lives. Prayer is a practical discipline as well as a spiritual practice for those who desire to lead people to grow and serve.

Enthusiasm

You do not need to fake excitement for the things of God if you understand the enormity of what He has done by the pardon of your sins and the privilege of serving the God of the universe! Are you excited about what God has done for you? Are you passionate about your class and your place of service? Are you excited about what God is doing and is going to do in your congregation? If not, then why should anyone else be?

Vision

What do you see God doing in your class or group in the next year? Is it going to be business as usual or are you anticipating that God is going to work in a greater way? What would your class be like if everything came together in a way that pleased God and completely fulfilled the purpose of the group? What is your vision? Does your class know what it is? Why should anyone want to serve if nothing is going to be accomplished or nothing is going to change?

Verbalization

The vision has to be communicated. The members of your class cannot read your mind. In addition, you have to express it over and over. Some members will not take it seriously at first. Others may not be present the first time that you share it. Yet others may not be ready to receive it at this point but may be later on. Share your vision on many occasions as you teach and communicate with your class.

Appreciation

Most people do not want to be screamed at, but they do want to be appreciated. You are serving alongside other volunteers. They do not expect financial compensation, but they often desire simple acknowledgment. Desiring appreciation is a part of human nature, and you have the currency to make the payment. Publicly acknowledge when members volunteer to help. Give members titles and place their names in writing in class and church publications. Send thank you cards and offer eye-to-eye expressions of gratitude. When someone knows they are appreciated and that their efforts were not unnoticed, they are often willing to go the extra mile for the person who is gracious in their acknowledgment.

Personal Commitment

Followers are unlikely to exceed the commitment level of the leaders. If you are strolling into the room five minutes after the advertised beginning time, teaching a half-hearted lesson, missing several weeks out of the year, neglecting to share a vision for your class, and/or failing to be fully involved in the life of your church, your chance of motivating anyone is nonexistent. You will have a class of passive attendees who do not grow, do not serve, and may drain energy from the life of your church. You have a responsibility that is also an opportunity. People who observe your strong level of commitment realize that they have the potential to step up to the plate also. You do not have to be perfect, and you cannot. However, your level of commitment must be high or you disqualify yourself in the eyes of your followers.

You must see the organization of your class or group as an opportunity and not a burden. The time you invest in organizing and equipping others to serve will cost you time in the early stages but will save you time and multiply the investment of ministry, service, and sharing that will come out of the class in future months. It enhances the prospect of the lost being reached as more members take responsibility for serving instead of just sitting through weekly Bible study and worship.

It is easy to complain about people being uncommitted. Do not be a defeatist! God has called you to lead. Where there is leadership there will be followship. The result will be that lives will be changed. Serving God is essential to the growth of believers. It is a component of making and becoming a disciple. As you enlist and engage your members to serve in your class or group, many will be called by God to serve in other areas. Now you are really making a difference. The influence of your leadership and of your class extends into the church and into the community as leaders are sent. Organization is not an add-on to your responsibility but an opportunity to make a difference.

DISCUSSION QUESTIONS

1. What are the commitments and expectations of the Sunday school leaders in your church? What adjustments need to be made to these moving forward?

2. How can you encourage your Sunday school teachers to be more effective leaders?

3. How is it that you are best motivated by other leaders? How can you improve in your motivation of those whom you lead?

4. How well organized are your classes? What adjustments and improvements need to be made organizationally?

CHAPTER 6

A Sunday School That Really WO_RKS . . .

Reaches Out to the Lost and Unchurched

JESUS SAID, "THERE WILL BE more joy in heaven over one sinner who repents than over ninety-nine just persons who need no repentance" (Luke 15:7). Do you believe that? I know that I do. It not only causes joy in heaven; it also brings great joy to families, to congregations, and to Bible study groups. Nothing quite compares with being acquainted or in some way involved in seeing a person come to know Christ. The joy multiplies when an individual, a congregation, or a group is blessed to see several people come to know Christ.

What would happen in your church if more than twice as many people trusted Christ as Savior in the next year as you were blessed to experience last year? It probably sounds like a tall task. Please be assured that it would bring great joy to God and the angels in heaven. Do you think it would be possible for God to do that? I believe that the same Spirit who brought three thousand to faith on the day of Pentecost is still at work in the world today. Bringing ten to faith instead of five or thirty instead of fifteen is not a tall task to the Holy Spirit. The question is, are we willing to position ourselves for God to bless in such a way? I do believe that only God can save, but I equally believe that the Scripture teaches believers to witness and that He works through the witness to bring people into a relationship with Him. A church has many opportunities at its disposal to be positioned for God to bring people to faith. Evangelistic preaching, personal witness encounters, intentional servant evangelism, market place evangelism, vacation Bible schools, revivals, crisis ministry, and intentional evangelistic events are just the tip of the iceberg. You will observe that congregations that are more intentional (i.e., position themselves) in engaging nonbelievers are blessed to see more people come into a personal relationship with Christ than congregations that are evangelistically passive. The same is true for groups within a congregation such as Sunday school classes and small groups. It is a reflection of the principle of "seed sowing."

The more seed that is sown, the more of a harvest the sower can expect in return. What would happen in your church in the next year if every Sunday school class or small group made a commitment to pray, strategize, and intentionally seek to bring two people to faith in Christ and to be baptized? First, I believe that God would bless the effort since He Himself desires to bring people into a personal relationship. Second, I believe that it is attainable because any group of ten (which is the average size of a Sunday school class or small group) could experience this blessing if they were intentional about it. Third, I believe it would bring great joy to every congregation and class as well as to the angels in heaven. What would be the result for your church? Do the math. Multiply the number of classes/groups in your church by two. Compare that with the previous year's baptisms. We discovered in our state convention that baptisms would increase by 166 percent in the average church if every class or group led two people to trust Christ and be baptized.

Consider the Great Commission once more: "Go therefore

and make disciples of all nations, baptizing them in the name of the Father and of the Son and of the Holy Spirit, teaching them to observe all things that I have commanded you; and lo, I am with you always, even to the end of the age" (Matt. 28:19–20). What is it that you are to be teaching? You are to teach everything that He commanded. Would that not include the responsibility to reach out to the lost and unchurched? Dr. Charles Roesel, retired pastor of First Baptist in Leesburg, Florida, once said: "People do not tend to drift toward evangelism, but to drift away from it. Leaders must continually call the members back to evangelism." Sunday school classes will not ordinarily engage in reaching out to the lost and unchurched unless they are led by someone to do so. How can you lead your class to reach out to the lost and unchurched?

GETTING PAST FEAR OF THE "E" WORD

Go ahead and face it. It is true. Most of the members of your class have a fear of evangelism. They may view evangelism as a verbal confrontation with a stranger or going house to house to engage people they do not know. Perhaps they are afraid that they will be asked questions that they cannot answer. Or sadly it may be that sharing their faith in Jesus is the last thing on their mind. They have received forgiveness of their sins and entered into a relationship with the Son of God. At the same time they have insulated themselves from the reality that the community is filled with those who are lost and separated from God because of their sin. Could it be that you have the same fears?

Many believers understand evangelism to be the responsibility of the minister. "Isn't that what he is paid to do?" He does have a responsibility to proclaim the gospel, but remember that he does not have contact with everyone. You and the members of your class or group come into contact with people day in and day out that the pastor or staff never have conversations with. The Great Commission is not a pastoral commission but a command to all believers. Pastors have a responsibility for modeling evangelism and for training the members (see Eph. 4:11–16; 2 Tim. 4:5).

Have you ever walked down a dark road or through an alley late at night all by yourself? That can be scary as your mind plays tricks on you and makes you think the worst. Walk down that same road at the same time of the evening with eight or nine of your closest friends. It is amazing what those numbers do to your fear. Instead of fear there is joy as you talk and laugh together on the journey. The power of ten people is greater than the power of one. How might you take advantage of that power as you seek the greater power of the Holy Spirit in turning your class into a Bible study group that not only grows in their faith but also shares the gospel and has the joy of seeing others trust Christ as their Savior? If you can do that, you will be the leader of a Sunday school class that really works.

THE POWER OF TEN

How is it that you can lead your class to reach out to the lost and the unchurched? First, you should be prayerful. The book of Acts says of the early believers, "And when they had prayed, the place where they were assembled was shaken; and they were all filled with the Holy Spirit, and they spoke the word of God with boldness" (Acts 4:31). Begin praying for your class and with your class that God would use your group to bring people into a personal relationship with Him.

Secondly, you should be purposeful. If it were automatic it would already be happening. You must intentionally lead your class or group to reach out to the lost and unchurched. Your class is uniquely gifted to reach out to those who are in a similar life stage. Enlist others to help you and make your strategy a part of your group discussion on a regular basis.

Thirdly, you should be persistent. Reaching out to the lost and unchurched is not a one-time event or an occasional announcement that you make. You must sow the seed of the gospel message as often as possible. The more seed that is sown by your class, the more fruit that your class or group will bear. Approach the challenge of reaching out using many opportunities and sowing throughout the year.

Fourthly, you should plan evangelistic opportunities. You are about to discover ten possibilities. You will notice that every one of them engages your class in connecting the lost and unchurched with opportunities to hear the gospel message. Following are ten ideas that you can implement to involve your class in reaching out to the lost and unchurched. The list is not exhaustive but should serve to give you several ways for leading your class to reach out.

Finally, you should lead your class to identify prospects. Prospects are members of your community who are not connected to a church. Begin compiling a list with basic contact information such as name, address, phone numbers, and e-mail addresses, as well as biographical information that might assist your class or group in praying and providing ministry to each person identified.

The reason for doing this is twofold. First, the prospect list serves as a prayer list for your class or group. Lead your class to pray for these friends and neighbors asking God to work in their lives and to use your class to encourage them to develop and grow in their relationship with God. Second, the prospect list serves as an invitation list. Whenever the class or church has a fellowship opportunity, event, or special service, the class should be sure to contact and invite all prospects. Guests will not be present unless they are invited. A greater number of invitations extended will result in a greater number of guests present and a greater possibility that someone will hear and respond to the presentation of the gospel. Be sure to gather this information in your church services as people visit your Bible study, when they attend church activities, and through the reference of members of your class or group.

Sunday school classes tend to be and ordinarily should be organized by life stages. Preschoolers meet together, children meet together, students meet together, college students meet together, young adults meet together, and so forth on through to the senior adult groups. Each group has knowledge of likes, dislikes, challenges, preferences, and activities that are inherent in the lives of their peers whether they are believers or seekers. Sunday school classes should serve as teams working together so that the lost can be reached through their witness. Team evangelism is a great way to maximize the number of members involved in obeying the Great Commission in the community. My staff and I developed a plan that challenges every Sunday school class to take responsibility for reaching and baptizing two people in twelve months. Engaging Sunday school classes and small groups in reaching out to the lost and unchurched has the potential to have a dramatic effect on your church and community. I want to share ten ways a class or group can get involved or be more effective in their evangelistic efforts based on the acrostic: POWER OF TEN.

Participate in existing church outreach

Does your church have a weekly outreach ministry or visitation ministry? Does your church provide evangelism training for members? Is your class or group taking advantage of outreach opportunities already in place? Be sure that your class is participating in the existing opportunities provided by your pastor and staff. If your church provides weekly visitation, then set up a rotation to insure that your group is represented each week. If your church is sponsoring an outreach event for your community, then be sure to engage your class in participation. If your church provides evangelism training for members, then be sure to encourage participation by members of your group. What if your church does not provide these avenues of outreach? In that case, you will need to be more proactive. Consider teaching an evangelism course to your class/group. Consider sending members to make face-to-face contact with your prospects and first-time guests. Consider organization of outreach opportunities sponsored by your class or group and open it up to other classes or groups to take advantage of.

For student Leaders: Challenge all of your students to participate in the existing opportunities provided by your pastor and staff. If your church does not offer a weekly outreach night, set aside one night every month where all of your students and workers make phone calls or personal visits. Consider sending your leaders to make face-to-face contact with your prospective students and first-time guests.

For children's leaders: Challenge all children's workers and parents to participate in the existing opportunities provided by your pastor and staff. If your church does not offer a weekly outreach night, set aside one Sunday afternoon every month where all the children, parents, and workers make phone calls or write postcards to prospects and absentees. Ask children to enlist their parents for visitation and outreach.

For preschool leaders: If your church is sponsoring an outreach event for your community, be sure to engage your leaders and class parents in participation. If your church does not provide these avenues of outreach, you will need to be more proactive. Consider sending your leaders to make face-to-face contact with your prospect families and first-time guests.

Offer several fellowship opportunities

No other group in your church will be as effective in reaching your affinity group as your class. For example, college students are best suited to reach college-age adults. The same is true of young adults, single adults, and senior adults in reaching others in their same life stage. Many unchurched adults will have no interest in attending your Bible study. However, your class can still make a connection, and the door can be opened to share the gospel. Lead your class to provide four to six fellowship opportunities each year. However, the aim is not merely the fellowship of the class, although that will be one of the results. The aim is to provide activities that will attract the unchurched. Discuss the following with your class or group: What types of activities do people in our community who are in the same age group or have the same affinity as our group members enjoy doing on weekends? Which of those might our class or group organize with the intent of connecting unchurched community members to our class (with the ultimate aim of connecting them to Jesus Christ through the gospel)? Would it be a camping trip? A tailgate party before the high school football game? A volleyball tournament? A car show? There are hundreds of possibilities. What works for your class or group may or may not work for another age group in your church or for the same age group in another community. The key question is not "What do we like to do?" The key question is "What do people in our community like to do?" You will discover plenty of activities that are wholesome and morally acceptable for your class. In order to make any difference evangelistically, you must keep the following in mind:

1. Plan several opportunities and place them on the calendar well in advance.

2. Pay attention to details and do the activity well.

3. Invite, invite, invite prospects. What is your plan to insure that a large number of people are invited?

4. Have a great time whether well attended or poorly attended.

5. Have someone share his or her testimony or a devotion and provide an invitation to trust Christ as Savior.

6. Invite them to future Bible studies and activities. Remember that a lack of response at the first event does not mean people cannot or will not respond in the future.

For student leaders: Discuss the following with your students: What types of activities do youth in our community enjoy doing on weekends? Which of those might our class organize with the intent of connecting with unchurched youth (with the ultimate aim of connecting them to Jesus Christ through the gospel)? Would it be a camping trip? A basketball tournament? A fishing trip? A flag football game? A girls' night? An all-night lock-in? What are other possibilities?

For children's and preschool leaders: Discuss the following with your leaders and parents: What types of activities do young adults with children in our community enjoy doing on weekends? Which of those might our class/group organize with the intent of connecting with unchurched adults and their children (with the ultimate aim of connecting them to Jesus Christ through the gospel)? Would it be a camping trip? A parents' night out? A volleyball tournament? A parenting class? A fishing trip? What are other possibilities?

Welcoming environment must be developed

What happens when guests show up for your Bible study or for your outreach fellowship? Are you ready to receive them and make them feel welcome? It is awkward to be new on the job, new in the community, or new in a church. Take time to evaluate and prepare your welcome for your Bible study hour and your fellowships. Here are some keys:

1. People must be present when guests arrive. How many people are present ten minutes before time to begin? Imagine being a guest and walking into a (nearly) empty room. Develop a greeter team and discuss with members the reason for arriving early: it is for the guests/unchurched.

2. Offer refreshments to your guests. It might be coffee, a soft drink, or snacks depending on the setting. This is common courtesy and a way to make visitors feel welcome.

3. Make nametags available for everyone. It is easier to remember names and much more inviting to be able to call people by their names. Do not assume your group is too small to need nametags. If even one guest is present, then nametags are a necessity.

4. Be sure the guest is engaged in conversation. Guests should never be sitting or standing by themselves.

5. Connect guests to class/group members with similar interests. Once you discover what they enjoy, you need to introduce them to others with similar interests. For example, if you discover they enjoy camping, introduce them to others in the class who are campers. These ideas are starting points.

Discuss with your class/group other ways to make the environment more welcoming and implement the ideas without delay.

Encourage members to be good inviters

Why do guests visit a class or group or participate in a fellowship opportunity? The answer is simple. They are invited by a friend or by a relative. Read Luke 14:15–26. Inviting is not a substitute for evangelism, but it is a credible supplement. Consider the following example: Group A invites forty guests to attend their fellowship. Group B invites six guests to their fellowship. Who will have the most guests? This is not rocket science, but the class/group members need to be reminded. Remember the aim. You want the unchurched to hear and have opportunities to respond to the gospel. Consider tracking the number of guests invited to your Bible study, fellowships, and special church events. You will discover that more people are present when more people are invited. Furthermore, when more are present there is a greater response to the gospel!

Reach out to people in crisis or transition

You do not wish a crisis on anyone; however, the reality is that all people experience crises in their lives. Did you know that most adults who trust Christ do so upon the convergence of two dynamics? First, they experience a crisis, and second, there is a Christian or group of Christians who minister to them during the crisis.[1] It is at this point that they experience the love of Christ through the ministry of the body of Christ and their hearts are open to the Holy Spirit. Consider the following exercise on the first Sunday of each month: Take a few minutes and ask the class/group to share prayer requests for unchurched friends and neighbors in crisis. Follow up by asking if there is one of those situations that the class/group members could assist or ease their burden during the crisis. Once you select an individual or a family, discuss specific actions your group is willing to take in the next month to minister during their time

---

1. Rainer, *Surprising Insights from the Unchurched*, 169.

of need. Follow through with ministry, love, compassion, and prayer. Begin seeking opportunities to share the gospel at the appropriate point.

For student leaders: Youth face transitions every year. They may be starting at a new school, or they are starting to date for the first time. Maybe their family has been through a recent crisis such as a divorce or separation. The common thread of each of these circumstances is crisis or transition. Consider asking your students to create a prayer list of unchurched friends and classmates who are in crisis or transition. Follow up by asking if there is one of those for whom the class/group members could assist or ease his or her burden during the crisis. Once you select a student, discuss specific actions your group is willing to take in the next month to minister during this time of need. For example, have your class write notes of encouragement and welcome to new students. Follow through with ministry, love, compassion, and prayer. Begin seeking opportunities to share the gospel at an appropriate point.

For children's and preschool leaders: Children face transitions every year. They may be starting school for the first time. Or maybe their family has been through a recent crisis such as a divorce or separation. What bigger transition is there in life than the addition of a new child? Do you know of families that are dealing with serious childhood sicknesses? Consider asking your children's leaders and parents to create a ministry list of unchurched friends and neighbors with children that are in crisis or transition. Another idea is to contact the local schools to learn of families that may be in a time of crisis or transition. After discovering the need, discuss specific actions your group is willing to take in the next month to minister during their time of need. For example, have your children write get-well cards to unchurched families with sick children. Another example would be to ask a group of families to specifically pray for and bring meals to an unchurched family with a newborn. Follow through with ministry, love, compassion, and prayer. It is at this point that they experience the love of Christ through the ministry of the body of Christ, and their hearts are open to the Holy Spirit.

Offer testimonies and gospel presentations at every opportunity

Some unchurched community members have no interest in sermons or in what your pastor has to say (with all due respect to your pastor). Your story, by contrast, resonates in a way that a sermon cannot. Be sure to allow group members to share salvation testimonies at fellowship events and regularly during your Bible study gatherings. It may be the message the Holy Spirit uses to enable an unchurched person to realize his or her need for Christ. Ask people to write their testimony and allow you to read it privately. Share with them your insights and then ask them to share with the group. It is always best to know beforehand what is going to be shared.

Focus on seasonal opportunities

Christmas, Easter, Mother's Day, graduation week, Independence Day, Valentine's Day, and Super Bowl Sunday. The days are not all the same and do not bear the same importance, but they do all have something in common. To be clear, none of the general holidays is remotely as significant to us Christians as the celebration of the resurrection of Jesus. However, what do they have in common in terms of evangelistic opportunity? Each of these special days attracts a larger than average number of the unchurched to gatherings of believers where the gospel can be shared. You and your group members can show up and simply enjoy. Or, since unchurched people would not ordinarily go to church or to a fellowship on a typical weekend, spend several weeks leading up to the holiday or activity focusing your class/group on praying, preparing, and inviting the unchurched to participate. Be sure that the gospel is shared and an invitation is extended. Should you do this for every holiday? Not necessarily. Discuss two to four holidays that your class/group members will concentrate on in the coming year. For the others, feel free to simply show up and enjoy!

For student leaders: Consider offering special youth events such as a Super Bowl party, Valentine's Day Banquet, or Christmas Dinner Café. Be sure to share the gospel and extend an invitation. Discuss with your class/group two to four holidays you will concentrate on in the coming year.

For children's leaders: Consider offering special children's events such as a Fall Festival, a community Easter egg hunt, or a children's music special. Your children's class/group can also partner with adult classes to help put on a Valentine's Day banquet or Super Bowl Sunday party. Be sure to share the gospel and extend an invitation. Discuss with your leaders two to four holidays you will concentrate on in the coming year.

For preschool leaders: Consider offering special preschool events such as an angel breakfast at Christmas, a community Easter egg hunt, or a baby dedication. Your preschool class/group can also partner with adult classes to help put on a Valentine's Day Banquet or Super Bowl Sunday party. Be sure to share the gospel and extend an invitation. Discuss with your leaders two to four special events that you will concentrate on in the coming year.

Teens and children are open to the gospel

What does openness to the gospel among youth have to

do with your class/group? Research consistently reveals that about 65 percent of people who trust Christ do so prior to their college years.[2] The challenge is leading your class/group to work together to see people trust Christ and follow in baptism. Ideally, the new believers will become affiliated with your class or group. However, do not limit yourself. For example, why not take vacation Bible school as a class project? Commit to serve, but more importantly, work together as a class/group to get un-churched children to participate. The reality is that several children could come to know Christ if a class/group is assertive in inviting and bringing children from their community. Likewise, consider the possibility of connecting with evangelistic youth events. The aim is not to bring children from other churches but to bring the unchurched. They are in every neighborhood, and they are often eager to participate if someone will bring them.

Equip class/group members to share the gospel

The members of your group need to be both prepared and available. Do they know how to share the gospel message with a friend? Do they know how to extend an invitation to respond? Take responsibility for equipping class members to share their testimony and to share a gospel presentation. You could do this on a given Sunday, as a series, or with written or recorded materials that you provide. Make sure to involve the entire class/group by equipping members during your weekly Bible study time. Materials are plentiful. Take advantage of what your church already offers. If you are not aware of possible resources, ask your pastor or a staff member, or contact your state convention or denominational evangelism ministry.

---

2. GeorgeBarna,"EvangelismIsMostEffectiveAmongKids,"2004,http://www
   .barna.org/barna-update/article/5-barna-update/196-evangelism-is-
   most-effective-among-kids.

New community members are seeking relationships

Do you know what it is like to move to a community where you do not know anyone? Many of you do. It is a fact that new neighbors are looking for relationships and assistance in acclimating to the community. Consider putting together a welcome basket from your class/group with gifts, community information, church information, and an invitation to your next class/group fellowship. Ask class/group members to identify one newcomer each month (giving particular attention to their own neighborhood). Deliver the gift and provide a warm welcome to the community. Offer to accompany a newcomer to the next scheduled Bible study or fellowship. You can either pick them up or have them follow you. If an event is more than a couple of weeks away, offer to take newcomers out to dinner. Go with two or three members or couples from the class/group and share the cost. You will be opening the door for people to come to know Christ if you are intentional and persistent as a class/group. In addition, you may discover your new neighbors are already believers who may contribute leadership to your class and church in the months to come!

LEAD THE WAY!

Evangelistic churches are led by evangelistic pastors. Evangelistic Sunday school classes are led by evangelistic Sunday school teachers. You do not necessarily have to be gifted in evangelism to be effective in reaching out to the lost and un-churched. However, you must have a conviction concerning its importance and necessity because of the extent of lostness in your world and community as well as an understanding that it is your responsibility based on the Great Commission. The key is to take responsibility and to lead the way. Your class or group members will follow your lead.

I recently led our staff to conduct research of the most effective evangelistic churches here in our state of Georgia. A few of the lessons that we learned are applicable to the leadership of your class. We asked the participants to share how their church was different from the other churches in their community. Twenty-five different responses were provided for this open-ended question. The most common response was given twice as frequently as the second most common response. The most frequent response was: "We are more intentional in our evangelism [than other churches in our community]."[3]

The June 2007 issue of *Facts and Trends* summarizes the findings of the top 22 of 43,000 Southern Baptist churches in terms of evangelistic effectiveness over the span of ten years. The article reveals that one of the five key factors in these churches is "intentional outreach." The article states: "Intentionality in evangelism is another common attribute among these churches. The pastors are focused on reaching people for Christ. Whether it's through focusing the content of sermons, planning the worship services, or simply the nature of church programming, it is clear that everything is designed with church outreach in mind."[4] Your class and your congregation must be intentional in reaching out to the lost and unchurched.

A second lesson we learned related to prayer. It is futile to attempt to be effective in evangelism without being effective in prayer. Every Sunday school class engages its members in prayer on some level. What is it that the class is praying for? The top evangelistic churches were asked to respond to the following open-ended question: "How does your church connect prayer to evangelism?" The most frequent response was given more than 50 percent more often than the second most frequent answer. The churches emphasized that they pray for

---

3. Parr, *Georgia's Top Evangelistic Churches*, 4
4. Libby Lovelace, "Standout Churches: Encouragement for Evangelism," *Facts and Trends* (May/June 2007): 9, http://www.lifeway.com/lwc/files/lwcF_corp_factsandtrends_07MayJune.pdf.

the lost by name. They pray for the sick, the hurting, members in need, for missionaries, for families, and for a variety of church and community issues. However, many congregations and Sunday school classes pray for the lost generally and, sadly, some may not intentionally pray at all for specific people to come into a relationship with Christ. The most effective evangelistic churches identify and pray for the lost and unchurched by name. Developing a prospect list gives you a source and an opportunity to engage in this important practice. In order for the lost to be reached, the class must pray for people by name.

We also noticed that the most effective evangelistic churches connected their ministries to evangelistic opportunities. Leaders of these churches understand that no ministry is inherently evangelistic. The ministries in the effective churches are similar to those that you will find in other churches. However, these churches approach their ministries in such a way that evangelistic results are the norm. The same ministries are often found in churches in neighboring communities but do not result in decisions for Christ or baptisms.

Leaders are often searching for that one ministry that will elevate evangelism in their church or class. But evangelistic effectiveness is not limited to one or a small number of exclusive ministries that are common to a large number of churches. The reality is that these top evangelistic churches found a way to make fifty different ministries evangelistic. Is it the ministry that makes it evangelistic or is it the approach to the ministry? It is the approach that the church or class chooses to take. A vacation Bible school can be evangelistic in one church and not in another. A class fellowship can be evangelistic in one church and not in another. Likewise, a revival, a women's retreat, children's worship, Sunday school, a softball team, a Christmas musical, and so on can be evangelistic in one church and not in another. It is not the ministry itself but often the approach of the congregation to the ministry that makes it evangelistic or keeps it from being so. You must be intentional in leading your class to connect your class fellowship and activities to evangelistic opportunities.

We also discovered that the top evangelistic churches connect their Sunday school and small group ministries to their outreach strategy. An overwhelming 90 percent of the top evangelistic churches responded that they strategically and purposefully make this connection.

YOUR SUNDAY SCHOOL CLASSES: HOUSEBOATS OR FISHING BOATS?

"When He had stopped speaking, He said to Simon, 'Launch out into the deep and let down your nets for a catch'" (Luke 5:4). I know you are familiar with this story. You may recall how Jesus got into Simon Peter's boat and pushed back a short distance from the shore in order to teach the multitude of people who had gathered. Following the message, He turned to Simon and asked him to take the boat into deeper water in order to catch some fish. Simon responded that they had already fished all night and were unable to catch anything. It is clear that Simon was tired (he had fished all night) and that he was frustrated (we toiled all night and caught nothing). Nonetheless, he deferred to the leader and headed into the deeper water. Do you recall the result of his obedience? The Scripture says that "they caught a great number of fish." They caught so many fish that their nets began to break and they signaled for their partners in the other boat to come and help.

In spite of his fatigue and frustration, Simon Peter launched his boat into the deep and went fishing. Here is a question that I want you to consider: Why did he do it? I am looking for the most elementary explanation. Here it is: He went fishing because his leader asked him to! I realize that there are a variety of possible answers, but this is the simplest interpretation. I believe this fishing account is literally true, but I also believe that it paints a picture of what the church is supposed to be doing. This story is illustrative of the Great Commission. Every church is a fishing boat that should be intentionally launching out into the deep (going) and letting down their nets for a catch. Likewise, every Sunday school class and small group is a fishing boat. Jesus said, "Follow Me and I will make you become fishers of men" (Mark 1:17).

One of the drawbacks to effectiveness in evangelism in our churches is that we have converted our fishing boats into houseboats. What do you do on a houseboat? You relax, fellowship, and enjoy the company of those on the boat with you. You do have work to do, but it is centered on maintaining an environment of leisure. You likewise have work to do on a fishing boat, but the objective is different. A fishing boat exists to assist you in catching fish. A Sunday school class or small group exists to help you to reach the lost and unchurched. It is organized around affinity groups to assist in this endeavor. Middle school students reach out to middle school students, college age young adults to college age young adults, senior adults to senior adults, and so on.

Why is it that some churches use their Sunday schools and small groups as tools for evangelism and others do not? It is because in some churches the leaders ask them to. Sunday school directors: are you challenging your classes to be fishing boats? Pastors: are you equipping your groups to go fishing? Teachers and group leaders: are you intentionally leading your classes or groups to reach out to the lost and unchurched? I want to challenge you to make a commitment to convert your houseboats into fishing boats. Here's the possibility of doing so: "For he [Simon Peter] and all who were with him were astonished at the catch of fish which they had taken" (Luke 5:9). I pray that this verse will reflect the testimony of your Sunday school in the years to come.

Do you recall the pattern of leadership that Jesus used to lead others to grow and serve?

- He summoned others to join Him.

- He took responsibility for their spiritual growth.

- He equipped them to serve.

- He sent them out to serve.

Do you recall how He went out into the community and took the apostles with Him as He shared the love of God? You have been called to do likewise. Lead your class or group to live what they are learning from you as you teach God's Word. Be intentional in leading your class to see the lost community around them, to pray for the lost and unchurched, to plan activities and opportunities to proclaim the gospel, and to get outside of the walls of the classroom and into the community. That is the way that the lost are reached, lives are changed, and leaders are sent.

DISCUSSION QUESTIONS

1. What outreach activities are currently being offered by your church? Which are most effective evangelistically?

2. What types of activities do the unchurched in your community enjoy that your class or church could provide as outreach opportunities?

3. Suppose your class or group members had an unchurched friend who lost his or her job. Discuss ways that your class or group could minister during their time of crisis. What other common types of crises should your class be aware of in looking for opportunities to reach out to the unchurched?

4. Are the classes or groups in your church more like houseboats or fishing boats? What are some ways to help your members and leaders to be more effective in evangelism and outreach?

CHAPTER 7

A Sunday School That Really WOR<u>KS</u>...

Keeps All of the Members Connected

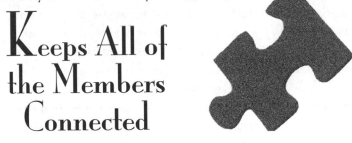

I HAVE THE UNIQUE PRIVILEGE of working with hundreds of Sunday school leaders and pastors every year. God has blessed me on my journey to be involved with churches where the lost are being reached, lives are being changed, and leaders are being sent. I have the joy of teaching others how they can have the same experience through the ministry of their Sunday schools and small groups. It is thrilling to speak with pastors and teachers once they begin applying principles that make a tangible difference in their ministries. Here's one letter that I received:[1]

Dear Steve,

About two years ago a young woman, Tina, began to attend our couples class and later ask us to pray for her husband, Greg's, salvation. Greg had grown up in our church but had

---

1. Only the names have been changed.

never accepted Christ. He had been away from church for years and would not attend with her, even when their little girl was in a program. Our class began to pray for him.

Some of the members in our class work at the same job as Greg and began to purposefully reach out to him. Shortly thereafter, he started attending whenever his daughter was in a program. He started having some health problems, and our class and his co-workers let him know that we were praying for him. A few months ago he agreed to be enrolled in our class but wanted to know why we wanted to enroll him since he never attended our class. We shared with him that we cared for him and wanted to help him in any way that we could.

Slowly he began to ask questions about spiritual matters, and his wife shared that she could see God working in his life. About two months ago he began attending and has not missed a Sunday since he started. He said, "I don't know why, but now I want to come." We know why! Seeing our prayers answered energized our class. We now have a list of unbelievers that we are praying for.

We began to pray even more fervently for his salvation. We rejoiced when his wife told us that he had accepted Christ although he was hesitant about making a public profession. The pastor and I visited him and gave him the option of sharing his decision at his baptism service (rather than responding to a public invitation during a church service). He said, "No, I want to respond publicly during a worship service, and I want my co-workers to go with me." We all rejoiced when he did. Greg will be baptized on Easter Sunday.

Here is an example of a class that really got it. Here is a Sunday school class that really works. When I talk about growth, that is what I am talking about. You see in this letter that the lost were being reached, lives were being changed, and leaders were being sent. "I tell you that in the same way, there will be more joy in heaven over one sinner who repents than over 99 righteous persons who don't need repentance" (Luke 15:7 HCSB). I know what some of you are thinking. What about the members of our class and church? What about their needs? Jesus is the best example at this point. He was the master of ministry, and He clearly balanced ministering to the needs of His flock while also seeking out the lost, but He did do both. I find that many Sunday school classes totally neglect seeking out the lost. You almost have to overemphasize it in order to produce the needed balance.

However, if you neglect to minister to the needs of your class members you will not have anyone to partner with in reaching the lost, and you will not have any leaders to send. You must keep all of the members connected. You do that by building relationships, meeting ministry needs, and helping them to grow in their faith. The Sunday school has some tools that can help you to do that. You may have heard of some of them, but you may or may not know how to use them to your greatest advantage in staying connected to all of the members. Take a fresh look at some tools that have been around a while and see if you are using them to their maximum potential.

THE ENROLLMENT TOOL

Your enrollment is a tool that can be used to keep all of the members connected and has the added benefit of serving as a growth tool. Almost every teacher keeps a roll book or computer-generated list of some type, but few know how to use it to its greatest advantage. You have a list of names that you keep in a book or on a computer printout that have been assigned to you over the course of time. Perhaps you have added some names and deleted others as time has gone by. Many teachers view their enrollment or class roll as a list of people who attend the class. The most common approach is to add them to the enrollment if they attend and to remove them once they stop attending. You may be surprised to discover that this approach is the reason that many Sunday schools do not experience growth. Please note that I have yet to find any Sunday school that has experienced sustained growth while failing to utilize enrollment in any form. How can you use your enrollment to keep all of the members connected while also strengthening attendance?

You begin by adjusting your definition of enrollment. If you view your enrollment as an attendance list, you have a closed system. You make it hard to get on to the Sunday school roll and easy to get off. In order to keep connected to all of the members you will need to view your enrollment as a ministry list rather than an attendance list. Your roll does not consist of people that attend your class; it is a list of people that you are committed to minister to. You need to establish an open system. You should make it easy to get on to your Sunday school roll and hard to get off.

What happens when a person is enrolled in your class or group? First, he or she receives intercession. The roll book or sheet serves as a prayer list. Each person on your roll can be prayed for regularly whether that person attends every week or rarely attends at all. You may want to resist keeping someone on your roll who rarely or never attends. Suppose it is one of my daughters who once attended regularly and is now struggling spiritually. At what point do you suppose that I want you to stop praying for her and ministering to her? The answer is never. Second, a person who is enrolled receives invitations. He or she is regularly invited to participate in fellowship opportunities where meaningful relationships can be developed. The list is a reminder of who needs to be invited and included in fellowship and ministry opportunities offered by your class and congregation.

Third, a person enrolled in Sunday school experiences

involvement. He or she is regularly encouraged and reminded to participate in Bible study that strengthens his or her relationship to God, to family, and to kingdom service. A person enrolled not only receives ministry but also is involved in ministry to others as he or she engages in Bible study and worship opportunities.

Fourth, those enrolled in Sunday school have inclination. He or she is challenged and much more likely to volunteer for ministry, to engage in evangelism and outreach, to participate in private and public worship, and to grow in his or her faith than a person who is not enrolled in Sunday school.

Adopting an open approach to enrollment provides the avenue that you need to keep all of the members connected. How can they stay connected if you remove them from the roll because they no longer attend? Once someone is removed from your roll, you have severed the intercession, invitation, involvement, and inclination of the former member. Could it be that people stopped attending because they were not receiving ministry? Enrollment is a ministry tool and a growth tool, but the tool must be used. If you cannot find a way to minister to every person on your roll, you will not be able to stay connected to all of the members.

Is there ever an appropriate time to remove someone from the roll? The answer is yes. You respond based on the most effective definition of enrollment. Enrollment should be viewed as a list of people that you are committed to ministering to. Therefore, it is appropriate to remove someone from the roll once you can no longer minister to the person. You will primarily encounter four circumstances that negate your ability or need to continue ministry. The first is when a person moves out of your community. I encourage you to go the extra mile at this point by contacting a church in the person's new community and giving the church contact information so ministry to the individual or family is not disrupted. Second, you will want to remove someone who joins another church. Even if the church is in your community, it is appropriate to remove the person who has communicated by actions a desire to receive ministry from that specific church. Third, it is obviously appropriate to move someone from the roll who has passed away. Finally, you would remove someone from your class or group roll in the rare circumstance where the person personally requests that you do so.

Beware of the temptation to purge your roll of members who no longer attend. You have no guarantee that they will attend in the future, but you are practically guaranteeing that they will never attend again if you cease to minister to them. Maintain contact and ministry with those on your roll so long as they remain in your community. You may ask, "But what about my percentages? It lowers the percentage of people present in my class each week." Remember that ministry is about people, not percentages.

In some ways the person who is not attending is in more desperate need of prayer, ministry, and fellowship than the person who is attending regularly. I acknowledge that it is frustrating to have people on your roll who never attend or give any support. However, if your class or group will maintain contact, pray for them, and minister in their time of crisis, you have an opportunity to reconnect in the future. However, do not let your roll get cluttered with former members who have moved away or have joined other congregations. It is acceptable to audit your roll, but please resist the temptation to purge instead of doing the work of ministry.

At what point should you add someone to your enrollment? Should you invite people to enroll on their first visit or should you wait until they attend three times in a row? To answer this question, refer to the definition. If the roll is a list of people that you are committed to minister to, you add them at the point you can begin ministry. An open enrollment approach is one where you may enroll anyone, anywhere, anytime, so long as they agree. New members to the church should be added to someone's roll automatically in order to ensure that someone has responsibility for ministering to them. Are there people in your worship service that do not attend Sunday school and would match the affinity of the class that you lead? Invite them to enroll in your class even if they do not attend. Ask them if you can add them to your group in order to pray for them, to invite them to your fellowships, to provide ministry, and to give them opportunities for Bible study. Point out that you would like to do this for them whether they can attend or not. Notice that you are making the commitment. He or she will most likely agree to be enrolled if this is your approach. Once you begin praying for people, inviting them to your fellowships, and providing ministry, they are much more inclined to attend your Sunday school class than they were when they were not on your roll.

Most of the churches that I work with that have growing Sunday schools take this approach. They have a system of enrollment that is open. Notice the differences in open and closed enrollment systems listed in table 7.1.

Your enrollment enables you to keep connected to all of the members because you know to whom you have ministry responsibility. Churches that choose not to have an enrollment have a huge ministry gap in their church. That same gap can be found in a church with rolls if you do not intentionally use them as a ministry tool. In addition, a proper approach to enrollment can also enhance growth.

The following two statements are equally true: First, increasing the enrollment will not automatically ensure an increase in attendance. Second, you will not experience sustained growth in attendance without increasing the enrollment. Allow me to illustrate this on a churchwide scale and then follow by showing you how increasing enrollment can increase the weekly attendance in your class.

I was assisting a church in evaluating their Sunday school and trying to identify the barriers to their growth. The church in this case had been blessed in the previous decade to baptize an average of twenty-five people each year in addition to adding a few more people by transfer of membership. Some of those who were baptized were children and students, but altogether the church added about thirty new people to the membership each year over those ten years. At the same time, some of the members had passed away and a few members had been lost along the way, but the membership had a net increase of a couple hundred. However, the Sunday school had not experienced growth; enrollment was the same (within about twenty) as it was ten years earlier. This church did not practice open enrollment, and new members were falling through the cracks because they were not connecting, finding relationships, or receiving ministry. The pastor could not do it by himself, and the Sunday school leaders were not trained to do it. This example illustrates how a church may experience surges of growth but will not sustain growth in the Sunday school without expanding the enrollment.

Now here's another example. Which of these three churches will have the higher attendance next Sunday: (1) a church with 45 enrolled in Sunday school, (2) a church with 220 enrolled in Sunday school, or (3) a church with 700 enrolled in Sunday school? The church with 700 enrolled is going to have more people in Sunday school, more people involved in the music ministry, more leaders, and a greater missions offering on Sunday morning. Why? They have more people to draw from. You cannot shrink your enrollment and grow your Sunday school attendance. Nor can you keep your enrollment at the same level and experience sustained growth. Think about it. A church cannot average 75 in Sunday school attendance if only 45 are enrolled! The total enrollment of the Sunday school in your church has a major influence on the average attendance.

You must be intentional about expanding it if you want to see more of the lost reached, more lives changed, and more leaders sent.

Table 7.1. Open Versus Closed Enrollment Systems	
Open Enrollment	**Closed Enrollment**
The roll is a ministry list.	The roll is an attendance list.
Easy to get on the roll, hard to get off the roll.	Hard to get on the roll, easy to get off of the roll.
Leaders are assertive about increasing the enrollment.	Leaders are passive about enrollment.
Anyone may be enrolled at any time so long as they agree.	A person may enroll by showing some level of commitment (such as attending three times in a row).
The class is committing to the person enrolled (to minister).	The person enrolled is committing to the class (to attend).
A person remains on the roll as long as the class can provide ministry.	A person remains on the roll until they stop attending regularly.
New members and believers are automatically assigned to a class (enrolled).	No one is added until he or she attends.
The leaders assign as many of the members who live in the community as possible to a class in order to provide ministry.	Members are on rolls only if they attend regularly.
Almost every member receives ministry.	Only faithful attendees receive ministry.

Let's see how this principle affects the attendance in your class. In our state, Georgia, 49 percent of those enrolled in Sunday school are present on an average Sunday. That percentage has been the same for decades. It may vary in some regions, some congregations, and some classes but will generally range from 40 to 60 percent for most. Remember that some people will be absent each week due to illness, travel, family emergencies, and lower levels of commitment. If everyone who attends showed up on one Sunday, the percentage would obviously be a lot higher. You may average a much higher percentage of attendance to enrollment in senior adult classes and younger preschool classes. You will likely average a much lower percentage with college-age classes and single adults (because they are gone more weekends). But if you add enough classes together it will average out to around 50 percent.

For the sake of illustration, let us assume that you have eighteen enrolled and you average eight in attendance. You are not likely to average fifteen out of eighteen in your Bible study. You may have fifteen attend on a special day, but you are not going to average fifteen out of eighteen. Why? You will always have six, eight, or ten people who cannot be there for the reasons previously shared. Suppose you want to average fifteen each week. If that is the case, you will need to lead your class to regularly minister to about thirty to thirty-five people. That means you need to expand your enrollment from eighteen to thirty. You need to enroll and minister to twelve additional people. Do you think you might be able lead your class or group to identify, enroll, and begin ministry to one additional person a month for the next year? If so, your enrollment will expand to around thirty, and if you will keep connected to all of the members on the roll, you will likely average around fifteen in your Bible study. Why not do it?

Be aware of the following: if you increase your emphasis on ministry but do not expand your enrollment, you will be ministering to the same people, and the attendance will not increase. If you increase the enrollment but fail to minister to everyone on the roll, the enrollment will inflate, but the attendance will not increase. The key to using enrollment as a tool to stay connected to all of the members while increasing attendance is to expand enrollment and regularly minister to all of the members. You must lead your class to provide the ministry in order to keep all of the members connected.

THE CONTACT TOOL

How would you feel if you missed church several weeks in a

row and no one noticed that you were absent? How would you feel if your family was going through a crisis and no one from your church acknowledged it or offered support in any form? How would you feel if you visited a new church and no one acknowledged that you were ever there? If you are like most people that I know, you would be hurt or maybe offended. I can provide many examples where this has happened, and I imagine that you can too. How does it happen that a person is absent for a long time, goes through a crisis, or visits a church and goes unnoticed?

I have asked the following question to hundreds of pastors: Have you ever had a member of your church hospitalized for several days and you failed to visit or call the person because you were completely unaware that he or she had ever been hospitalized? Almost every pastor will tell you that this has happened at some point along the way. It was not his fault! No one let him know what was going on. Your pastor is not psychic, and if he is he should not be a pastor! The pastor cannot keep up with everyone and everything that is going on. What if the church was broken down into groups between ten and thirty with each group assigned a leader? What if that group met each week for Bible study but also had the responsibility of ministering together and ministering to one another? The groups could maintain regular contact with one another and whenever there was a crisis they could respond and take responsibility for communicating with the pastor and staff the status of any crisis situations. If only there were an avenue through which the church could implement such a plan. There is! It is already in place. It is called the Sunday school. It can be accomplished when every class or group understands it to be one of the responsibilities of the class and is intentional in implementing a contact ministry.

A contact is an intentional communication on behalf of the Sunday school class through phone calls, electronic communication such as e-mail, social networking, personal visits, cards, or wayside encounters. The purpose of the communication can include, but is not limited to, inviting someone to attend the Bible study, inviting someone to attend a fellowship or special event, making follow-up contact with a recent guest, calling someone who was absent, sending a card acknowledging a special occasion in someone's life, or ministering to someone in need. Preventing the scenarios where people and situations go unnoticed is a simple matter. The class or group must maintain regular contact with every person who is enrolled. The contact is the way that you discover ministry needs, determine how to provide the ministry needed, and keep all of the members connected. People will get connected when they are noticed, when they receive ministry, and when they develop relationships with others in the class or group. Once they connect, they are more inclined to attend, participate, and serve. It is easy to complain about the lack of commitment that the members of the class have while neglecting to lead the class to do the very things that connect them and help them grow, especially to the point where they desire to attend the class and serve its members. The teacher must lead the class or group to ensure that the following three things happen:

- Any first-time guest to a Bible study or fellowship gets follow up contact within seventy-two hours.

- Anyone who misses the Bible study gets a personal contact within the next week.

- Every member, regardless of frequency of attendance, receives contact at least a couple of times each month to determine ministry needs.

How are you going to do it? The first possibility is to take personal responsibility. If you have a small enrollment and the time required, you may personally follow up new guests, contact the absentees every week, and call every person or couple enrolled at least a couple of times each month. Most teachers do not have time to accomplish this task. Do you choose to neglect it and let ministry needs go unmet? Taking personal responsibility is exactly what you must do if you teach preschool or children. Enlisting a coleader for your class is critical in order to spread the responsibility and increase the consistency. Do not assume that you do not need to maintain contact with infants or toddlers. Your aim is to maintain contact with the parents to discover and respond to ministry needs as well as to enhance relationships. Adults and student classes have no excuse at this point. All the members as well as the leaders are capable of sharing the load.

Therefore, you have another option. Involve others in the class in making the contacts. Perhaps you could enlist a team to follow up those who visit the class and those who attend your fellowships. You could also enlist an individual or a team to contact those who are absent on Sunday. Likewise you could take time at the end of the class to make assignments to the members that are present. Yet another option is to personally take time to follow up first-time guests and develop a care group ministry to make regular contact with members to address ministry needs and follow up absentees.

A care group ministry is a strategy that can enable your class to maintain contact with every member. You begin by enlisting one care group leader for every four to seven people or couples enrolled. A care group leader has the following responsibilities:

- Contact each person or couple assigned to your group immediately to introduce your ministry and to gather biographical information.

- Share a meal with each person or family assigned to your group as soon as possible.

- Attempt to contact each member assigned to your group each week and ask for prayer requests in order to identify ministry needs.

- Report ministry concerns to the teacher and pastor while maintaining confidentiality when appropriate.

The teacher or an assigned care group coordinator should contact each care group leader later in the week to receive their prayer requests and to assist in following up on ministry needs discovered. Care groups will not work on autopilot. The teacher or a care group coordinator must train the care group leaders and maintain regular contact with them for encouragement and accountability. When assigning members to the care group leaders, it is advantageous to assign members to leaders where relationships already exist. You may notice that you have nonattending members who do not have relationships in the class. In that case you have identified the reason they are not connected and do not attend. Someone from the class must take responsibility to initiate regular contact and develop a relationship with them.

The weekly attendance in your class is greatly influenced by the number of contacts that are made by the class or group members. Encourage every member of your class to make contacts each week by inviting people and ministering to one another spontaneously as well as through organized means. Ask members to write down or share the number of contacts made in the previous week and add the total together. You will begin to notice that attendance is higher when contacts are greater and attendance is lower when contacts are fewer. Try it for ten or twelve weeks and you will see for yourself. I challenged a church where I served as interim pastor to aim for three hundred contacts in one week. The goal was to attempt to contact and invite every member and every prospect three times in one week to attend Sunday school the following week. The Sunday school average attendance was sixty-five. The congregation was thrilled to see more than one hundred in attendance the Sunday following the week of contact emphasis. Why did almost forty extra people show up for Bible study? The answer is because so many more people were contacted, invited, and ministered to that particular week. I led the congregation to begin tracking contacts, and it became obvious that weekly attendance was influenced by the number of contacts made each week. You have to teach your class, spend time in your class, and lead your class to utilize the contact tool if you want to keep all of the members connected.

You will need to be observant and intentional in leading your class to respond to ministry needs as they are discovered. You will hear of many ministry needs as you take prayer requests each week prior to your Bible study. Every prayer request is a ministry need for someone. Often you will find that the need is for someone or some issue that is outside of your community or realm of influence, in which case the actual prayer is the only response needed from your class members. However, the request may present an opportunity for your group. Consider these five prayer requests as examples: "Please pray for my aunt who lives out of state as she has surgery next week." "My husband will be laid off and out of work beginning next month." "Pray for my wife who is out today with the flu." "Pray for my husband to come to know Christ as his Savior." "Pray for the earthquake victims in Japan." Suppose each of these requests were shared in your class. You should certainly lead your class to pray for these needs. In addition, at least three of these requests could be doors of direct ministry opportunity for the class. Your group may be the answer to their prayer. Share these sample prayer requests with your class, or provide some similar examples, and discuss how a class might respond by providing ministry. You may be surprised how simple responses make such a huge difference in the lives of those touched and how it affects participation and attendance in your class.

THE FELLOWSHIP TOOL

I recently attended a neighboring church that had a dynamic worship service. The music and the message were delivered with excellence. The congregation was enthusiastic and the experience was exciting. I cannot express enough how much I appreciated the quality, the investment, and the energy that went into the preparation and the presentation of the service. However, no one spoke to me personally! Yes, an usher shook my hand as he gave me the worship bulletin, and a few people smiled and shook my hand during a fellowship chorus, but no one asked me my name. No one introduced themselves to me. No one engaged me in any meaningful conversation. It probably happens in your worship service too (at least on occasion). I am honestly not sharing this as a complaint but in order to make a point. Relationships are not developed during the worship service. A worship service is designed primarily to enhance a person's relationship with God.

A small group environment is somewhat more advantageous. Getting noticed is easier in a group of ten to twenty than in a group of one hundred or more. Developing relationships is also easier in a Sunday school class or a small group than a worship service, but it is not automatic. I want to say that one more time: it is not automatic. The way to keep all of the members connected is by building relationships, meeting ministry needs, and helping them to grow in their faith. You can help build relationships by developing fellowship inside and outside of the class itself. Establishing a contact ministry will help, but it will not meet all of the relationship building needs.

The environment of the class itself as it meets on Sunday morning can be an asset or a liability to relationship building. I was invited to visit a church anonymously as part of a consultation to evaluate the strengths and weaknesses of their Sunday school. I arrived about ten minutes before starting time and was directed to a welcome center. A gentleman identified an appropriate Bible study class for me to attend and ushered me directly to the room. I was impressed by how organized the welcoming process had been up until this point. I arrived in the room at the exact advertised starting time of the Sunday school hour. The welcome center usher left me in the room and explained that the teacher would be there soon. I was a first-time guest, and I was left in a room all by myself. Five minutes later the teacher of the class arrived. It was a long five minutes for me as a first-time guest in a new environment. The teacher was personable, and we engaged in conversation for the next ten minutes. Actually, there was no other choice. The first member of the class arrived fifteen minutes after the advertised starting time. I was introduced to the members, and soon the Bible study proceeded. Every member shook my hand and smiled. However, none of the members engaged me in any meaningful conversation.

The teacher did an excellent job in his presentation of the Bible study and interacted with the class through good discussion. The class was dismissed, and I had no clue where the worship center was. I followed the crowd and found my way. I received no follow-up communication from the class. I want you to notice something at this point. The Bible study itself was good. However, I would have had no interest in attending that class again if I were searching for a new church home or if I were an unbeliever who happened to visit. The class made no attempt and was not prepared to connect with me on a personal level.

You may think that it does not matter that much what time the members arrive or how prepared you are to receive guests because you rarely or never have any. The reality may be that you rarely or never have guests because you are not prepared to receive them. I want to invite you to take time to study James 2:1–9 to be reminded of how the congregation should treat guests. You will learn that all guests should be honored and that no one should be treated with partiality. Every guest is a potential leader for your class or group in the future. Every guest may potentially have a great impact on the life of your congregation. Some guests may not have a personal relationship with Christ and may form opinions about Christ and the church based on their experience with and in your class. The environment and the attitude of your class is not a trivial matter. The teacher must take responsibility for modeling, equipping, and leading the class to be intentional in receiving and seeking to develop relationships with every member and every guest. You are not responsible for their response, but you are responsible for your efforts or lack thereof.

Are you familiar with the "climate principle"? The climate principle states that there are things you do not have to do, but if you do them they will make a difference. Take a quick journey into two hypothetical Bible studies. As you arrive at the first one, no one is there other than the teacher. The members roll in over the course of twenty minutes, the Bible study proceeds, and you are not personally engaged by any of the members. The first Bible study is like the one I described previously. The following week you attend another Bible study. Several members are standing around as you arrive. You are offered some coffee or refreshment and immediately you are conversing with other people about your family and your community. Everyone has nametags, and you are spared the embarrassment of forgetting someone's name after several introductions. Someone discovers that you are into camping and immediately introduces you to another member with the same enthusiasm, and you are quickly swapping stories. You are invited to sit with him and his wife, and the Bible study begins. The Bible study is of the same quality, no better and no worse, than the one you experienced in the previous setting. The couple you are sitting with asks if you would join them in worship, and they would count it an honor to take you to lunch after worship. Although you cannot go, you are appreciative that they made the offer. It does not end there. The couple asks if they might have your phone number in order to call and arrange an opportunity in the next couple of weeks to have you over to their home or to take you out to dinner. You receive the call on Monday evening and the arrangements are made. Would I be too presumptuous to suggest that most guests would be more responsive to the second Bible study?

The quality of the Bible study itself was no different. What was different? It was the climate that was created by the second group. Do you have to have members arrive early to receive guests? No, but it does make a difference. Do you have to have refreshments or coffee? No. Do you have to have nametags? No. Do you have to invite guests to sit with you or to go out to lunch? No. Do you have to be intentional in introducing people who have similar interests? No. But if you do these things, it will make a difference. You should take an opportunity to discuss this question with your class: what are some things that we do not have to do, but if we do them, they will make a difference in making guests feel welcomed?

A small group Bible study hour has an advantage in developing and building relationships over a worship service environment, but there are still limitations. How much conversation can actually take place during that hour? Time has to be made for announcements, prayer requests, and most of all for the Bible study. You typically only have from five to fifteen minutes of interaction built on personal conversations. You need not apologize for creating and providing that time. It need not take anything away from the Bible study, which is ultimately enhanced as the climate improves and more people desire to participate. You should purposefully provide additional fellowship opportunities for your class or group in addition to the Bible study itself in order to encourage greater development of relationships.

The teacher or the leader of the class will have to address the issue of time and leadership again at this point. Take time to enlist a fellowship coordinator or team. Be assured that someone in your class loves to entertain and plan social events. Serving in this role is a great way to wed their gifts with a meaningful ministry opportunity. A weekend gathering on a Friday or Saturday evening creates and expands the conversation opportunities from a few minutes to a couple of hours. You can accomplish more relationship building in one fellowship gathering than in several weeks of Bible study. Keep in mind that more people will attend the Bible study if they have relationships, which provides the opportunity for you to help them grow in their relationship with God. Fellowship gatherings can have an indirect influence on seeing that lives are changed and can have a direct impact on the lost being reached. Whenever fellowship opportunities are created, the class should take advantage of inviting and including people who have little or no interest in attending the Bible study. With minimal extra effort, the group can reach out to the lost and unchurched without sacrificing the fellowship that they enjoy as they gather.

How often does your class gather for fellowship? Once will not do, because not everyone will participate. Twice would be better, but you will still miss some members. Whenever you gather for a fellowship, you can assume that not everyone will participate. Some will not attend because of other obligations at the time of the fellowship. Others will not attend because they have no interest in the specific activity that is planned. The class should plan several fellowships throughout the year as a group and should vary the types of activities that will take place. One person might respond to a golf outing where another will attend a Valentine's weekend dinner. Offering a variety of activities opens the door to a greater variety of participants over the course of the year. The person who rarely or never attends the Bible study may attend the fellowship because of interest in the specific activity. While participating, that person will interact and potentially develop relationships that connect him or her to the class. The likelihood of attending the Bible study increases because of participation in the fellowship. Some of you will object at this point that people should be more committed to spiritual activities than social interactions. The reality is that those who do not have a relationship with Christ are not spiritual, and even some members may be struggling spiritually. The fellowship not only strengthens the relationships of the class members but also serves as an avenue to connect those who have less spiritual interest, with the ultimate aim of seeing lives that are changed.

Josh Hunt proposes that the frequency of fellowships should be monthly. He encourages classes to invite every member and every prospect to a fellowship every month. The aim is not to burden the class but to open doors of opportunity. He reminds leaders:

> If we want people to believe that God loves them and accepts them, we must love and accept them.
>
> In practical terms, this means spending time with people. It means inviting them into our homes and going out to dinner with them. We party with the people we love. We will work with anyone, but we spend casual time only with the people we care about. The greatest gift we can give someone is ourselves and our time. If we were half as effective at crossing social barriers as we have been at crossing theological barriers, we would have won the world years ago. One reason we haven't reached our country and our communities for Christ is that we simply do not love them. If we loved them, they would come. But they will not cross the barriers; we must go to them. Note that Jesus tells us to "*go therefore and make disciples*" (Matthew 28:19). We must take the initiative. We must do the going.[2]

---

2. Hunt, *You Can Double Your Class*, 64–65.

Lead your class to love others through frequent fellowship opportunities beyond the Bible study hour. In this manner you are also realizing that leaders are being sent as your members are purposeful in their participation with and invitation of guests. Equip your members to be spontaneous as well as intentional. Emphasize the importance of inviting guests to sit with you in worship, making follow-up contact with guests, inviting guests to lunch following the services, and seeking opportunities to share fellowship meals and recreational opportunities with new and recent guests. Teach your members that they may or may not bond with those whom they fellowship with, but they may recognize hobbies or experiences of newcomers that might serve as an avenue to connect them with other members who have similar interests.

WHAT IF THE CLASS HAS GROWN TOO LARGE?

Can you imagine being in a class of newborn infants through two years of age where seventeen are present? Yikes! How would you like to have responsibility for forty seventh-grade boys on a Sunday morning? A class can be too large to manage. You are in trouble if you expect to care for seventeen babies or forty middle school boys with only two adults. You must have more leaders, and you need more classes or units.

Hosting forty adults or seventeen college students would not cause the same concerns. You do not have the same concerns for safety, security, or behavioral issues. But the question is, can you meet the ministry needs of forty adults? The reality is that if even twenty-five are present, you likely have more than fifty enrolled. The real question is whether or not you can effectively minister to all fifty. The Bible study hour is not a concern so long as you have adequate space, but the ability to contact each one regularly, to develop a personal relationship, and to meet ministry needs is a tall task for a volunteer Sunday school leader. It may not be a matter of your ability but of the availability of your time and energy. I do not object to some adult classes being large, but if all of your adult classes are large, you will find that many ministry needs are being neglected and the back door grows wider and wider. Please note that larger congregations tend to have slightly larger classes. But the further you stray from healthy ratios of leaders to learners, the more difficult it will become to minister to your members and to assimilate new members and guests.

When is a Sunday school class too large? I do not provide a number in answer to this question, because the answer differs according to the leader. Some leaders do have the skill and more time to minister to larger numbers of people than others. One such leader is no more spiritual than the other but may be in a life stage that affords more time to invest in the ministry of the class. In any case, here are some indicators that a class is too large:

- The teacher of the class does not personally know each person enrolled.

- The group is too large for everyone to participate in discussion or group activities.

- The room is filled to capacity on a regular basis.

- More than fifteen people are attending on a regular basis, but less than 40 percent of those enrolled are present on average.

When less than 40 percent of those enrolled are present, it is often an indication that the class is struggling with maintaining contact, ministry, and care for all members. I have attended classes in which thirty, forty, and even more than fifty were present in a Sunday school class. You will always find a skilled communicator in classes of this size, and it is easy to take pride in drawing such a large number to a Bible study class. What if a class of thirty in attendance has eighty on the Sunday school roll? That is often what you will find in large classes. A volunteer will be hard pressed to minister to eighty people. Yes, there are exceptions, but you must honestly ask the following suggested questions before you assume that you fall into that group:

- Do you know all eighty of them?

- Are all members receiving contact from your class on multiple occasions each month?

- Are absentees automatically contacted the following week?

- Do all of the members have personal relationships with someone in the class?

If the answer is yes to all four, carry on and keep up the good work. But keep this in mind that since your class is so strong, it should be the greatest source for your church leaders to draw from when needing new teachers and leaders to serve in other areas. Be sure that you continue to focus on the lost being reached and lives being changed without neglecting the need for leaders to be released!

What do you do when the class is too large? The first option is to place a greater emphasis on your organization and on the implementation of a care group ministry. That may enable you to provide the ministry needed in addition to the excellent Bible study you provide. The other option is to release some of your members to create a new class.

Do not panic at this point. I do not believe in splitting

classes. However, I know this with absolute certainty: your Sunday school cannot grow by thirty, forty, fifty, or more people without creating some new classes. Why not? Because if you add fifty more people in average attendance to your existing classes, that means you have enrolled and begun ministry to over one hundred more people. The teachers that are in place in your church, as wonderful as they are, cannot keep up with and minister to one hundred more people. You will need four or five new classes and eight or ten new Sunday school leaders. Where will those leaders come from? They all come from adult Sunday school classes.

The reason that many Sunday schools do not grow is because they get stuck at this point. The adult teachers place the fellowship that they have developed and that the regular attendees are experiencing above the greater purpose of the class. Remember that the purpose is to enable the church to strategically embrace and engage the Great Commission. That happens when the lost are being reached, lives are being changed, and leaders are being sent. Keeping all of the members connected requires the building of relationships, meeting ministry needs, and helping members to grow in their faith. Creating new classes provides the avenue to simultaneously meet the ministry needs of the members while making room for new members as you reach out to the lost and unchurched. A study of more than three hundred churches that experienced a turnaround from decline to growth revealed that adding classes was a key component in their resurgence. Here is what the researchers learned:

> First, comeback leaders had an intentional process or strategy for small groups and/or Sunday school. Second, a status quo did not exist. Changes were made. Whether these comeback churches added, replaced, or started new classes, leaving this area of ministry the same was not an option. Third, comeback leaders utilized a training system to develop leaders for

small groups or Sunday school. Fourth, comeback churches worked to create more space to accommodate new classes or groups.[3]

Replicating your class is a compliment to your leadership. I am amused when teachers get upset because a Sunday school director or pastor approaches them about releasing members to start a new class. They will sometimes go and complain to the class members that the pastor is "trying to split my class!" Once the teacher grumbles and complains, the followers fall in step. You have just communicated to your class that you have no desire to reach the lost. That may not be what you meant to say, but that is the result of holding on to your class just like it is. The reality is that teachers often get upset when the pastor or minister of education has just given them a pat on the back. If you wanted to replicate a class, would you choose a healthy or an unhealthy class to help you in the process? Do you think that your pastor is going to go to a teacher and say, "Brother Bud, I noticed that your class is as dead as a hammer. Do you think you could help me to replicate that?" Your leader would not do that. You get approached to create a new class because you are doing a good job. You ought to hug his neck and lead your class to rejoice over this compliment.

Creating new classes can help the Sunday school to maintain groups that are manageable in relation to ministry responsibilities of the teachers so that they can keep all of the members connected. In addition, new classes reach people that the existing classes never did. It is the equivalent of twenty people fishing from two boats on two different parts of a lake instead of all fishing from one boat. You can catch fish either

---

3. Ed Stetzer and Mike Dodson, *Comeback Churches: How 300 Churches Turned Around and Yours Can Too* (Nashville: Broadman & Holman, 2007), 150–51.

way, but you can catch more fish if you divide into two boats. Every time you create a new class, you are launching an additional boat that will catch fish on different parts of the lake that the existing boats can never get to. In order to keep all of the members connected and to enhance the opportunity to reach out to the lost and unchurched, consider starting a new class when the following indicators are present:

- The age span of the class is too wide (more than three years for preschool and children, more than three grades for youth, and more than fifteen years for adults).

- The room is overcrowded.

- An age grouping is not being reached (e.g., college-age students).

- A special need can be met (e.g., Nearly Wed or Newlywed Class)

- When less than 40 percent enrolled attend a class of fifteen or more.

- The congregation desires to grow and reach more of the community.

Think back to the example that Jesus provided. He called his disciples, helped them to grow spiritually, equipped them to serve, and then released them. You are not supposed to have the same seven people sitting at your feet for ten years. The seven that you are teaching two years from now may be seven new people, and the seven that you are leading now may by then be serving in other areas. It may appear that your class has not grown, but you and I know differently. More importantly, the Lord knows. You truly have a class through which the lost have been reached, lives have been changed, and leaders have been sent. The kingdom of God has grown and your church has grown because of your unselfish leadership. May your tribe increase!

DISCUSSION QUESTIONS

1. What has been the approach to enrollment in your church? Class? What adjustments can be made to utilize it as a tool for growth and ministry?

2. What percentage of your members is not connected? How can your class and church be more intentional in connecting people to your congregation and class?

3. What are some ways that you can maximize the number of ministry contacts made by your class?

4. Discuss several ways that a class could respond to each of these needs: "My husband will be laid off and out of work beginning next month." "Pray for my wife who is out today with the flu." "Pray for my husband to come to know Christ as his Savior."

5. What are some wholesome activities that unchurched members of your community would be willing to do alongside believers if they were provided by your congregation? How could you maximize the possibility of guests being present? How could you connect those attending the activities to opportunities to hear the gospel?

CHAPTER 8

A Sunday School That Really WORK<u>S</u> . . .

Sharpens the Skills of the Leaders Continually

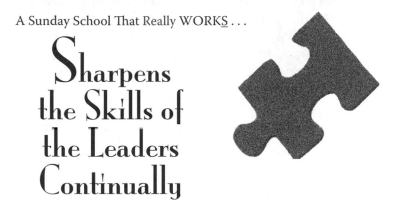

WHAT DO YOU DO IF you have the desire to be a more effective leader but do not have the time? Sunday school teachers are the busiest leaders in the church. Leading a class requires a strong commitment in order to prepare and present a meaningful Bible study each week. Where do leaders find the time upon taking on the additional responsibility for organization, leadership, outreach, and ministry? Most Sunday school teachers serve on teams and committees, sing in choirs or praise teams, and take on a variety of other responsibilities in the life of the church. All of these are volunteer roles in addition to family and work responsibilities.

You can take heart in the fact that it can be done. God will not call you to do anything that He will not equip and enable you to do. You could choose to do the minimum or just go through the motions, but that is not the type of person you are. You have been called by God to serve Him in a manner that will make a difference in the kingdom. No service for God is unimportant, and there is no doubt that Sunday school leadership plays an important role in the health of your church and the growth of the kingdom of God. You will need to sharpen your skills if you desire to be effective. Paul reminded Timothy: "Therefore I remind you to stir up the gift of God which is in you" (2 Tim. 1:6). You have been called by God and gifted for your place of service. That is what God has done. Now you have the responsibility to "stir up the gift of God which is in you." You have the responsibility to grow and sharpen your skills in order to fulfill what God has called you to do. You do not need to feel overwhelmed, and you do not need to give up. You need to grow. Here are four ways to help you find the time.

HOW DO YOU FIND THE TIME?

Prioritize

Leading a Sunday school class puts you in a position to make a real difference in the lives of the members and everyone whom they touch. You cannot do everything that you are asked to do at church or in your personal life. It is time to ask yourself what will make the most difference in the kingdom of God. Your personal relationship with God must come first. Your responsibility for and ministry to your family must come second. What can you do that will make the greatest difference for God once those two priorities are in place? You may have to let go of some less important activities and responsibilities in order to provide the leadership needed in the Sunday school. You cannot serve on several teams/committees and lead or participate in several organizations within your church. You may need to let go and let others serve in those positions. What if leadership is lacking in the church? Remember at this point where leaders come from. Almost every leader comes from an adult Sunday school class. People who attend worship only are not as inclined to serve as those involved in small groups. When you lead a Sunday school class effectively you are helping build the leadership base for your congregation. Make that investment a priority.

Practice (teacher) time management

Time management skills come easier for some than others depending on personality and giftedness. You can attend seminars and read books that provide thorough instruction on time management techniques, and I would encourage you to do so if it is a point of great need. Consider the following four ideas as examples of how to maximize the limited time that you have available.

1. *Utilize class time for organization.* The best time to meet with your class and with leaders is when you have them all together. It is appropriate to spend about a quarter of your meeting time each week for fellowship, administration, and organizational functions. You will still have sufficient time for Bible study. You might also consider spending half of the meeting time once every four to six weeks for a Leadership Day. Spending time with your class in planning and organization is the way that you lead the group to work together to apply as a group what you have been teaching from God's Word.

2. *Take advantage of Sunday lunch.* I am in the habit of eating lunch each and every Sunday. How about you? Meet with class leaders, teams, and/or potential leaders for lunch on Sunday. Taking one Sunday each month to meet with key members will add up to an investment of twelve to eighteen hours over the course of a year and will not infringe on any of your personal time.

3. *Preview the next lesson by Monday.* Take fifteen to thirty minutes by the time you go to bed on Monday to preview the Bible study for the following Sunday. What is the key passage? What is the lesson aim or objective of the study? What is the key application? Read the key passage alongside

your devotion each day. Once you get into the preparation of the Bible study or lesson you may be surprised how much work your brain has done during the course of the week as you prayed, processed, and meditated on the upcoming presentation.

4. *Utilize technology for meetings.* Do you need to meet with a team or an individual to plan or organize some component of your ministry? Does it require face-to-face interaction or could it be done some other way? Some tasks can be done by e-mail, by phone, or by some other means of electronic correspondence. These means allow participants to save the time of driving to the meeting and can eliminate some of the extraneous conversation in order to maximize time. Be wise and determine when personal gatherings are needed and when other means will suffice.

Put together a team

You cannot do it by yourself. You must take the time to enlist someone to help you. If you struggle with organization, you may want to enlist a class administrator or coordinator. If you struggle with evangelism, you may want to enlist an outreach leader. If you struggle with making time for ministry during the week, you may need to enlist a care group coordinator. What if you spend ten hours of effort over the course of a month to enlist and orient someone to assist you? What if that person in turn invests two hours each week in ministry and assistance over the next fifty weeks? Can you imagine that? You will have one hundred volunteer hours to supplement your ministry. Multiply that by three other leaders supplementing your work. That would be three hundred hours of volunteer service that resulted from a ten-hour investment on your part. Some of those hours will reduce the time required of you. Invest your time from the beginning in enlistment and equipping and you will be pleased to discover how much ministry work your class achieves and how effective your leadership has become.

Participate in training opportunities

Your pastor or other Sunday school leaders are promoting a training session in the near future. You are hesitant to participate because you do not believe that you have the time. It is not that you cannot be there but that your time is crunched by a variety of personal and church responsibilities. What if you knew that the hour of training that you were going to attend would enable you to be involved in reaching three unchurched or lost people? What if you knew that the training would enable you to save Bible study preparation time while improving your presentation? What if you knew that the training would equip you to involve others in a way that would save you forty hours in the next year while getting more ministry accomplished? That is the potential of every training session that takes place. Training is not a waste of time but an opportunity to learn skills that make you more effective and more efficient as a leader. That may not happen in every training opportunity but may be exactly what occurs when you choose to miss. You cannot attend every training session, but you should participate when you are available.

THE GREATEST INFLUENCE ON GROWTH

Did you know that one issue determines the likelihood of sustained growth or lack thereof of a Sunday school? The issue is whether or not your church provides training for its Sunday school leaders. You may recall the 2001 study of the fastest growing Sunday schools in Georgia cited earlier. The research revealed that the most common factor among these churches was that they provided training for their teachers and leaders. The churches were all sizes from small to large, and they accounted for 42 percent of the gain in Sunday school attendance and 15 percent of the baptisms in the year of the study, though they comprised only 1.3 percent of the churches.[1] Further research revealed that congregations that provided at least four training sessions per year experienced a gain of more than 11 percent in attendance over a three-year span while those that provided no training declined by 2 percent during the same period of time.[2] Training is the greatest influence on the growth of the Sunday school and is also a tremendous influence on whether or not you personally grow in your skills as a leader and a teacher.

Training is a systematic approach for conveying necessary skills to leaders that permit them to effectively carry out the ministry to which God has called them. Sadly, many churches enlist Sunday school teachers, assign them a room and a class, provide them with some form of curriculum, and send them to do the work of ministry without ever receiving any substantial instruction. Sunday school teachers need orientation and instruction even if they happen to be professional educators. I personally never received any instruction on conducting outreach, enlisting leaders, ministering to absentees, creating new units, or exegeting Scripture while I studied for my bachelor's degree in education. I have been leading Sunday school in some way for more than twenty-five years, and I am still learning new things. The reason that many Sunday schools struggle is that they have wonderful people enlisted to serve who have not been equipped with the skills needed to be effective.

Thom Rainer's research revealed that Sunday school was a common strategy used by churches that were effective in winning people to Christ. He makes the following observation in his study of effective evangelistic churches: "Training was a major factor for Sunday school leadership in these churches."[3]

1. See table 3.1 on page 63.
2. Crites, "Sunday School/Open Group Ministry."
3. Rainer, *Effective Evangelistic Churches*, 94.

Trained leaders will almost always surpass untrained leaders in effectiveness. Churches that provide training for their leaders tend to be more effective in reaching the lost and assimilating them into small groups.

The church teaches matters that bear eternal significance. The leaders of today's churches have a biblical mandate to equip those who minister in and through the church. Paul reminded believers in Ephesians 4:11–12 that "He Himself gave some to be apostles, some prophets, some evangelists, and some pastors and teachers, for the equipping of the saints for the work of ministry, for the edifying of the body of Christ." Equipping the members of the body to serve effectively is not a suggestion. Equipping those who lead preschoolers, children, students, and adults in Sunday school and small groups is imperative. Churches that experience sustained growth find a way to equip their leaders. I often hear pastors and staff make excuses for why they cannot get their leaders involved in training. I know that it can be done from personal experience as well as from my observation of so many churches that make training a priority and find a way to engage their leaders.

Ed Stetzer and Mike Dodson conducted a study of more than three hundred churches that made a turnaround after experiencing many years of decline or lack of growth. A renewed focus on small groups or the Sunday school ministry was a common denominator in the ability of the churches to reverse the trend of decline.

> Surveys indicate the importance of a small-group structure in connecting people to the life of the church and providing a place of ministry for church members. There was an increased emphasis on building community and an expansion of the number of groups offered. To support these new groups, teacher training became a priority. One comeback leader indicated that an increased emphasis in Sunday

school and increased teacher training were important factors in their comeback experience. The training gave teachers a clear set of priorities and showed them how to treat Sunday school classes or small groups.[4]

Other resources are available that detail the how-tos of leadership training. I want to add three words of encouragement at this point.

First, do not allow the number of participants present in your training to determine whether or not you will provide it. I believe that the Scripture mandates equipping and that you train the trainable.

Second, you do not necessarily have to meet with your teachers every week in order to be effective. I would suggest that you meet with your teachers at least four times a year while making it your ultimate goal to meet eight to ten times during the year. The times and places will vary from church to church. Some leaders will meet weekly on Sunday nights, others will meet for breakfast every other month, and others will meet monthly on Sunday evenings. The common denominator is not the time or the exact frequency. The key is to be systematic or to have a strategic plan for equipping.

Third, do not meet for the sake of meeting. Be sure to provide or participate in something that will energize your leaders and equip participants to be more effective in their ministry. The result will be more enjoyment on the part of the teachers as they lead the Sunday school ministry. Sunday school leader equipping is not an add-on but a strategic element in experiencing growth. Your leaders learn the principles of growth and leadership as they participate in training opportunities. If the principles occurred by osmosis, then everyone would be applying them and all Sunday schools would be healthy and

---

4. Stetzer and Dodson, *Comeback Churches*, 149–47.

growing. Provide and participate in the best equipping opportunities that you can, and if you have responsibility for leading it, ensure that the quality is as good as the Sunday morning worship experience or better. Effectiveness will not be accomplished in one session or one weekend of training. Sunday school leaders must commit to participate throughout their ministry in order to continually "stir up the gift of God" that is within them (2 Tim. 1:6).

The pastor, Sunday school director, and staff members who lead educational ministries should plan and promote training for the Sunday school leaders. Plan at least four to ten training sessions each year and place them on the church calendar at times when nothing competes for participation. The time may be the same each month or may vary. The key is to give leaders a complete plan on the front end. You will elevate the importance of the training sessions and encourage leaders to place these opportunities on their calendars well in advance by providing a twelve-month plan. The plan could also include options such as reading, viewing video training at their convenience, or attending additional conferences off location.

Plan to have time for inspiration, instruction, and information. Do not spend the entire time going over administrative issues and announcements. Provide inspiration through testimonies, music, devotions, and acts of appreciation. Spend the bulk of the time on instruction, providing the leaders with skill development. Teach a combination of skills requested by the teachers along with skills that the Sunday school leadership understands to be critical to the health of the Sunday school ministry. The instruction may come from video resources, teaching the principles from a chapter in a book, or creating a lesson to help teachers enhance or develop a specific skill.

The equipping sessions can be conducted at a variety of times including over breakfast prior to Sunday activities, over lunch following Sunday activities, or during Sunday afternoon.

In addition, a midyear banquet with a guest speaker, a Saturday retreat on or off site, or participation in a conference hosted by another church or organization could be included. The key is to promote the opportunities, expect participation, provide childcare if possible, and include the extras such as light snacks or a meal depending on the time of the training. Who should lead the training? It should be the person who is skilled at communicating. It may or may not be the Sunday school director. The quality is so important to the success of the training. Do it well and your leaders will look forward to it. Do it poorly and you will struggle for participation. Let me add one other important note about training your leaders. You do not provide training based on the number of participants. You provide it based on the biblical admonition to "equip the saints" and in view of the fact that it affects the health and potential growth of the Sunday school more than any other factor. Don't neglect to train a few even if the majority appears to resist. Make it a priority, do it well, and watch your leaders begin to grow and make a difference.

CRITICAL TRAITS OF SUNDAY SCHOOL LEADERS

A 1999 research project by George Barna sought to discover what church members look for in a leader. The top response (87 percent of respondents) was someone who will motivate people to get involved (see table 8.1). Church members are looking for someone to motivate them. A leader is one who intentionally challenges, inspires, motivates, and influences others to become involved in the task to which they are committed (or called). A coach motivates his or her players to practice and perform in an effort to win a contest against the opposing team. A general motivates his soldiers to prepare and perform in order to defeat an enemy. A business owner motivates his or her employees to plan and work in order to provide a product or service that will turn a profit. A Sunday school leader motivates his or her class to grow in and apply their faith in order to fulfill the Great Commission, which is in essence the church's mission statement given by Jesus Christ our leader. Those who lead you desire for you to be effective in your leadership of others. A Sunday school teacher who desires to be an effective Sunday school leader will need to possess and develop four specific leadership traits.

Table 8.1. What Church Members Are Looking for in Their Leaders

Ranking	Response	Respondents (%)
1	Motivate people to get involved	87
2	Negotiate a compromise when there is a conflict	78
3	Identify the course of action to take	77
4	Made decisions which are in the best interests of the people, even if those decisions might not be popular	76
5	Train and develop other leaders to help	75

Source: Information from George Barna, "Leadership, Self Defined, What People Want," http://www.barna.org/cgi-bin/PageCategory.asp?CategoryID=25 (accessed October 20, 1999).

First, your attitude is critical. You set the tone for the members of your class. Let us consider an example. Imagine that your class has an average attendance of seven and the room where you meet can accommodate about twenty. Down the hallway is a growing class that averages twelve in attendance in a room that will only accommodate twelve. What is the logical solution to enable both classes to have the room to grow? Your class needs to give up the room that you occupy so that both classes have room to grow. What is your attitude going to be? Are you going to grumble, complain, and pout in front of your class? Perhaps your class decorated the room or invested in some upgrades.

Which choice will best enable your church to fulfill the Great Commission? Clinging to the upgrades or making a sacrifice that will allow others to be reached? Your attitude is contagious, and you are the one who has control of it. Whether it is changing rooms, participating in a project, creating a new class, or promoting a corporate goal for the entire Sunday school, your attitude will influence the attitude of everyone in your class. Determine to never allow your attitude to be a barrier.

Second, your skills must be developed. Would you take your car to an unskilled mechanic? Would you go for a medical appointment to an unskilled doctor? Would you allow your child to attend school with unskilled teachers? What makes you think that people would want to attend a Sunday school class led by an unskilled teacher? You must be attentive to your teaching skills. You must continue to grow in your ability to communicate God's Word in an appropriate way to the age group and the audience to which you have been called, but the development of your skills cannot end there. Remember that you are the growth expert in your Sunday school class. Seek out and develop the skills needed to lead your class to reach the lost and unchurched. The skill is not automatic, or everyone would be doing it. Reading this book is one way that you can grow in your skill at leading your class to be effective in fulfilling the Great Commission.

Third, your cooperation is invaluable. You are going to experience situations when your pastor, Sunday school director, or minister of education wants you to be involved or lead your class in participation in some activity, promotion, or project. On some of those occasions they will be more excited than you are about the possibilities. You may even mildly disagree or lack enthusiasm for the endeavor altogether. Have you ever tried to lead a discussion where no one participated? Have you ever tried an outreach effort for your class and found yourself all alone in the effort? It is frustrating, is it not? Consider the motivation for which your leader has proposed the project or activity. More than likely the reason is founded on an effort to reach more people and/or to make the Sunday school more effective, which is certainly consistent with the intention of the Great Commission. If you refuse to participate, or even worse, if you criticize the idea to your class members, you are undercutting the credibility and leadership of someone who is sincerely trying to strengthen your Sunday school. If needed, go behind closed doors and share your perspective, but commit directly to your leader that when you go out the door you will support what they sense God has put on their heart to do. Which is worse: willing teachers with unwilling leaders or willing leaders with unwilling teachers? I will let you decide, but the sum of the matter is that neither scenario will position your congregation or your Sunday school to reach the community! Lead or follow, but never allow yourself to get in the way.

Fourth, your commitment level must be strong. This may surprise you, but did you know that some teachers choose not to show up on some Sundays and do not bother to make appropriate arrangements or make prior contact with their leaders? Did you know that some teachers arrive ten, fifteen, and even twenty minutes after Sunday school is scheduled to begin and think nothing of it? Did you know that some teachers go an entire year and choose not to participate in any of the training opportunities provided? No one is asking you to be perfect, but you are asked to be committed. "And whatever you do, do it heartily [passionately] as to the Lord and not to men" (Col. 3:23). How would it be different if Jesus were the Sunday school director? In a sense, He is! The members of the class are unlikely to ever exceed the commitment level of the leader. Give it your best, and you will get the best response.

THE TEACHER'S GROWTH

Does your church provide and encourage you to participate in equipping opportunities? You should be committed to full involvement if they do. Your participation affects your growth and models commitment to grow for those whom you lead. You can take personal responsibility for your growth even if not provided by your church. Effective leadership begins with a commitment to your personal spiritual growth. What is the most important thing that a teacher does each week? Is it planning outreach? Making ministry contacts? Teaching a Bible study? All of these are important, but they are not the foundation of your leadership. If you fail at this point of growth you cannot accomplish anything significant on any other level. The most important thing that you do as a teacher is to spend personal time with God each and every day.

Growing spiritually is not a mystery to you. You understand that you grow closer to God as you spend time in prayer, worship, and the study of God's Word. You must be careful at this point. You can get so busy doing things for God that you can neglect to spend time with God. Remember that you are a spiritual leader. Nothing that is proposed in this book is more important to you than developing an intimate relationship with God. That intimacy will give you the wisdom to set priorities, to clearly understand how to best invest your time, to teach with passion, and to lead others to grow closer to Christ.

You cannot effectively lead a class or group if you neglect your personal spiritual growth. It is like the foundation of a house. Do you remember what happened in Matthew 7:24–27? Two houses experienced a great storm. You recall how one house endured because it was built on rock while the other collapsed because it was built on sand. Neglecting your personal spiritual growth is like building a house on sand. You will not survive a severe storm in your life if you are not strongly rooted in your faith. The entire house collapses if the foundation gives way. Your entire ministry is subject to failure if your foundation is destroyed. Continually give attention to your foundation that should be built on an intimate relationship with Christ.

What is it that makes you want to hear a teacher teach? Think about it. Most people who answer this question would include passion or enthusiasm as an important trait of an effective teacher. Who wants to hear someone speak or teach who is dry, dull, or detached from what he or she is attempting to teach? Where does passion for teaching come from? It comes from spending time with God. The best teaching comes from overflow. Teaching is not easy, but it is easier if you are filled with the Spirit and passionate about what God is doing in your life. Spiritual growth affects every area of your life. Growing spiritually makes you a better mom or dad. It makes you a better spouse and a better parent. Spiritual growth affects your work and your relationships. Those whom you lead will not necessarily remember your lessons, but they will remember you! Will they see that you were authentic and that you had an intimate relationship with God that affected you as a teacher and made an impression on their life? Will they remember you as someone who fueled their spiritual fire or as someone they endured? You must grow in order to lead others to grow.

You cannot solely rely on your spiritual growth if you desire to be an effective teacher. Hundreds and thousands of teachers have an intimate relationship with God and yet struggle in leading their Sunday school classes to experience the lost being reached, lives being changed, and leaders being sent. The reason is that there is skill involved in developing leaders, organizing for growth, and effectively communicating God's Word. Have you ever known someone who really loved God but was boring as a teacher? I am sure that you have. He or she had an intimate relationship with God but did not possess the skills to instruct others about spiritual matters. That person's life may have been an example, but his or her influence was minimized because many people chose not to attend the class or group. Have you ever known someone who had an intimate relationship with God and possessed good teaching skills but never led his or her class to reach the unchurched? I imagine that you have. The person loved God but lacked the skills and the motivation to lead the class to reach out to the lost. It is at this point that many teachers miss the opportunity to be greatly used by God.

Some leaders believe because they have a close relationship with God that everything else will automatically follow. That is not necessarily true. You need to supplement your personal spiritual growth with the skills needed to accomplish the task to which God has called you. The skills vary based on the task. The skills that a person needs to serve on a finance team, to sing in a choir, to lead a recreation ministry, and to teach a Sunday school class all differ. Each needs to have an intimate relationship with God, but the skills needed are not the same. The spiritual gifts that the individual possesses may ignite the passion and provide an advantage, but that does not mean that they cannot learn from those who have already effectively served in similar capacities.

Paul often reminded Timothy of the importance of sharpening his skills. In 2 Timothy 1:6, Paul instructed Timothy to "stir up the gift of God which is in you." In chapter 2, he spoke of teaching skills when he said, "Be diligent to present yourself approved to God, a worker who does not need to be ashamed, rightly dividing the word of truth. But shun profane and idle babblings, for they will increase to more ungodliness" (2 Tim. 2:15–16). He follows in the third chapter by reminding him, "All Scripture is given by inspiration of God, and is profitable for doctrine, for reproof, for correction, for instruction in righteousness, that the man of God may be complete, thoroughly equipped for every good work" (2 Tim. 3:16–17). Being equipped for every good work is the aim of combining spiritual growth with skills growth. The skills come as the result of instruction provided by godly leaders. He continues in chapter 4 by challenging Timothy to develop a needed skill although it may not have been a personal area of Timothy's strengths or giftedness. He says, "Be watchful in all things, endure afflictions, do the work of an evangelist, fulfill your ministry" (2 Tim. 4:5). Timothy was challenged to develop the skill of an evangelist, implying that it was not a personal strength that he possessed. He had a responsibility to develop his skills as a minister as well as to grow in his relationship with God.

Your spiritual growth will enhance your skills and your spiritual gifts will fuel your passion to serve. Every ministry involves practical components that may or may not be addressed directly in Scripture. Christian leaders should never do anything that contradicts the teaching of Scripture, but they should not neglect the practical lessons and experiences provided by other godly leaders. Maximizing your potential as a Sunday school leader will require that you seek to develop Sunday school leadership skills as a compliment to your commitment to spiritual growth. You begin by committing to participate in any and all equipping opportunities provided by your pastor and Sunday school leaders. However, the neglect of leaders to provide training opportunities does not absolve the Sunday school teacher of his or her responsibility to stir up the gift of God that is in them.

OTHER TRAINING POSSIBILITIES

What options do you have if your church does not provide training? Even if your church does not provide training, you can take personal responsibility for your growth. As mentioned earlier the most important thing a teacher can do to build a foundation of effective leadership is by spending personal time with God each and every day. Through reading Scripture and praying to our Father in heaven, which can be likened to eating and breathing, the Holy Spirit nourishes your life in Christ and fills you as a vessel of blessing to others. You can also benefit from a number of other training possibilities that can develop your knowledge and skills and help you become a more effective leader and communicator.

Reading Books

Reading enables you to learn from leaders whom you may never have opportunity to meet. You have the advantage of reading at your own pace, and as an adult you will be pleased to know that no book review is due and no written exam will be required. You may think that you don't have time to read. Let me ask you a question. Could you read one to two pages each day? If so, you could read one to two books related to Sunday school leadership each year, and you can be assured that your skills will increase dramatically.

Observing

Take one or two Sundays each year to observe another teacher that you know to be effective. Follow up with an interview in person or over the phone and seek to discover what it is that makes that teacher effective. Be particularly observant and inquisitive of how they approach and apply themselves to areas that tend to be a point of challenge for you.

Experimenting

Most skills cannot be developed until and unless you put them into action. You must be willing to risk failure in order to discover what works and what does not. Do not be afraid to share with your followers that you are trying something new and do not be afraid to admit when you fail. In addition, do not discount something as ineffective simply because it does not seem to work in the beginning. Some skills require time and patience to develop.

Evaluating

You will have a difficult time developing the skills that you need unless you know what they are. Take time to evaluate the strengths and weaknesses of your class and of your leadership. Interview a trusted member of your group and ask for honest analysis. Have an experienced leader or staff member take time to evaluate your ministry. You may find that it hurts to have your weaknesses pointed out and exposed. But how will you grow unless you honestly know what they are?

Attending Seminars and Conferences

Check with your denominational leaders, with other Christian ministries, or with effective churches to discover what training opportunities they provide. An evening at a seminar or a weekend at a conference can serve to advance you to a greater level in your leadership. You may find that a cost is required. The investment has the potential to have a positive impact on many lives if it enables you to advance your skills.

Mentoring/Coaching

Ask a skilled leader to adopt you for a year to assist you in developing your skills. Determine together to meet every month for a year to discuss leadership issues relevant to your position as a Sunday school leader. Make a commitment to grow in your skills and to adopt a younger leader to assist in their development as you continue to grow.

Audio and Video Instruction

You can receive training in your own living room or vehicle. The time spent viewing or listening to training is flexible. You can begin at a convenient time, and you have the option of listening in whole or in part at any given time. Ask the leaders of effective churches if they record their training sessions and seek to get copies of the training for your benefit and growth. Digital recording and podcasting provide another avenue for skills training, which can give you an edge in your personal growth.

The skills that you need as a Sunday school teacher can be broadly divided into two categories. You need to seek continual growth in your leadership skills and in your communication skills. The leadership skills are the tools that you need to organize, enlist, and influence others to work alongside you in responding to the Great Commission. The communications skills are the methods that enable you to effectively prepare and present an age-appropriate Bible study for your class or group each week. The Holy Spirit works powerfully through your teaching and the application of God's Word to change hearts, attitudes, and lives. This book is devoted primarily to helping you to grow in your leadership skills. However, I do want to share a few brief ideas to assist you in your communication or teaching skills and will also recommend some specific resources that are devoted totally to helping you grow in this area along with others listed in the bibliography.

MAKING THE MOST OF LESSON PREPARATION

I have already shared two points that are critical to effective preparation of your weekly Bible study. First, be reminded once again that it is critical that you spend personal time with God each day. Your walk with God influences the way that you prepare and present the lesson to those in your class or group. Do you recall the observation made about Peter and John by the Sanhedrin in Acts 4:13? The Bible says, "Now when they saw the boldness of Peter and John, and perceived that they were uneducated and untrained men, they marveled. And they realized that they had been with Jesus." What a wonderful testimony! I pray that your class or group members will recognize that you have been with Jesus whatever your level of training. Teaching a Bible study should always be more than an academic exercise. The authority of the Scripture, the authenticity of the leader, and the ability of the teacher to communicate is a powerful combination. Spending time with God and growing in your relationship with Him are essential to preparation and enhance your presentation as others see Jesus working in your life.

Second, be reminded that preparation needs to begin early on. It is not essential that you complete preparation early in the week, but it is important that you begin preparation several days ahead of time. I want to acknowledge again that you are a very busy person. You may find yourself completing preparation for Sunday's Bible study on Friday, Saturday, or even Sunday morning in some circumstances. That may not be ideal, but it is a reality for a volunteer. You need to understand what I refer to as the "creative advantage." Creativity comes in proportion to the time that your brain has to process information. If you wait until Saturday to begin lesson preparation, you can get the job done but with minimum effectiveness. Preview your lesson as early in the week as possible. Take about fifteen minutes on Monday or Tuesday to overview next Sunday's plan, including the key passage, key application, and suggested teaching activities. You will find that ideas will come to you as you go about your routine of life in the course of the week. You might hear a news story that will serve as a good illustration for your presentation. A discussion with another teacher during the week may prompt an idea for an age-appropriate activity for your class to reinforce the main point. You may recall a personal experience from your past that would serve as a good example of a point that you need to make. A Scripture that you read may reinforce what you want to communicate. By the time you get to the actual preparation of the lesson later in the week, your brain has processed and developed several ideas that will enhance your presentation. The creativity that you will experience is a combination of spiritual insight and practical mental processes that will take your preparation and presentation to a new level of effectiveness.

Here are five more ideas that you can call upon to make you more effective in preparation.

Enlist a preparation partner

You can take two approaches to this strategy. The first is to enlist a member of your class to study the passage or lesson preparation material in advance of your preparation. Call them and spend time interacting about their insights and ideas to enhance your preparation. The second approach is to enlist a teacher who is teaching from the same curriculum or passage each week. Make a commitment to spend a few minutes in person or on the phone midweek to share insights and ideas.

Read the key passage each day leading up to your presentation

Do this in addition to or alongside your devotional time during the week. Consider taking time to memorize shorter passages. As you go through the week you can take opportunities to meditate on the key passage during quiet and alone times such as while walking or driving. You will open yourself up for the Holy Spirit to give you additional insight that you might never get when you prepare the day prior to the presentation.

Develop a preparation routine

Effective lesson preparation involves perspiration as well as inspiration. Remember to "be diligent to present yourself approved to God, a worker who does not need to be ashamed, rightly dividing the word of truth" (2 Tim. 2:15). Most of you serve in churches that provide curriculum resources to assist you in lesson preparation and presentation. Many hours of work are invested by the producers of the resources, and it saves you time. Do not assume, however, that the Bible study will prepare itself. You need to spend time in God's Word allowing the Holy Spirit to speak to you before you speak to others. Develop standards, disciplines, and routines to help you maximize your preparation time each and every week. You will have weeks when you are pressed for time. Develop a routine for preparation that spreads time across the week. That will allow you to compensate for those days that you are sidetracked and honestly have to miss the time you planned. If you put all of your planning into one time component or if you take a spontaneous approach, you will find yourself giving minimum attention to preparation.

Be sure that the message precedes methods

Methods are important tools that can help you connect the audience to the message you have been assigned. However, methods without a message result in nothing more than a social gathering. Discover and prepare a message to share that is based on the study of the Word of God. The younger the audience, the simpler the message will need to be. Commit to lead your class or group to look at, consider, and respond to the Scripture each week. You should follow by utilizing methods to maximize participation, understanding, and application of the message. Methods are important but are of no value without a biblical message in an environment of Christian education or discipleship.

Enjoy the privilege of preparation

Is your lesson preparation a chore or a privilege? I would estimate that about one of every fifty members in an average church is a Bible study teacher. Out of the whole community in which you live, you probably represent somewhere in the range of one out of one hundred. God has called you to this ministry of teaching. Do you realize how blessed you are that God in His infinite wisdom has selected you for this task? What a great privilege! I am sure that you are aware that you learn much more from preparing a Bible study or Sunday school lesson than you do as a participant. Let God speak to your heart at this point. Do not view your assignment this week or any other week as one in which you "have" to prepare a Bible study. I have good news for you. God has chosen you, and you "get" to prepare a Bible study. What an honor!

COMMON PRESENTATION MISTAKES TEACHERS MAKE

I also want to take the opportunity to share some thoughts about your presentation as well as your preparation. I have observed some common presentation mistakes in my ministry with Sunday school teachers. Here are ten mistakes that I want to encourage you to avoid.

Reading the Lesson to the Class

You should certainly read the lesson in preparation for the class. Please do not make the mistake of taking your teacher guide into the class and reading it to your audience or having them take turns reading various parts. You may think that it never happens, but it does. I hope you are not the one doing it. People do not come to Bible study to be read to. They can do that at home on their own. A new pastor was once fishing for compliments following one of his first sermons. He could not resist asking an elderly saint what she thought. She said, "Pastor, first of all, you read your sermon today. Secondly, you read it poorly. And thirdly, it wasn't worth reading!" Please do not read the lesson to the class.

Reading a Series of Verses and Asking, "What Do You Think?"

The question is not wrong or inappropriate in and of itself. Imagine a teacher who reads a verse and asks the class: "What do you think that means?" He or she follows by reading the next verse and asking the same question. The same pattern is followed for the next dozen verses with the same question being asked. It may appear that the teacher is seeking to be interactive, which is a positive communication goal. What is really happening? The teacher has not prepared. You can be assured that the members of the group realize that no preparation has taken place. The teacher has damaged his or her own credibility and may likewise undermine the Scripture itself if the audience misinterprets the passage because no one has really studied the background and meaning. Feel free to ask what the members think, but not over and over as the whole of your methodology.

Dry Lecturing

Did Jesus ever lecture? The answer is yes, and the Sermon on the Mount in Matthew 5–7 is a good example. Lecture is a legitimate method of instruction and is the root of preaching methodology. Let me ask you a question. Is the book of Revelation an interesting or boring subject matter for a Bible study? The way that I would answer the question is to say that it depends on who is leading the Bible study. Have you ever had a teacher or professor who spoke in a monotone voice with little or no enthusiasm or animation? Quite frankly this issue may be the reason that many people avoid Sunday school. I fear that many have attended and heard a presentation communicated purely through lecture that was dry and uninspiring. I have heard speakers like that, and I am sure that you have also. Be sure that you are not that type of speaker.

When and if you utilize lecture you should speak with passion and some animation. You need to speak up, speed up, and if you have more than a dozen in your audience, you may need to stand up. Be sensitive to the age of the audience. When leading a younger audience you will need to use lecture less often and in shorter increments. Also bear in mind that your learners only retain about 5 to 10 percent of what they hear. Combine other methods of engaging learners (such as involving the five senses of sight, sound, smell, taste, and touch) in order to maximize your effectiveness as a teacher no matter what age group you lead.

Ignoring Church Convictions

You need to be aware of a couple of points that affect your credibility as well as that of your pastor and church. You may not and probably will not always agree with every position that your church and staff take on issues of doctrine or methodology. You may need to address those concerns and will have to draw your own conclusions as to whether you can live with them or not. Learn to distinguish between essential doctrines, beliefs, and preferences. The essential doctrines are those biblical issues that are not open to compromise such as the literal and physical resurrection of Christ. Beliefs are those issues in which good men and women have differing views that do not disqualify the ability for worship and service together. Preferences are a matter of personal tastes, likes and dislikes, based on culture, upbringing, or personality that are not specifically addressed in Scripture. Some leaders make the mistake of elevating preferences to the same level as essential doctrines. They are not the same. Keep in mind the statement attributed to Augustine: "In essentials, unity; in non-essentials [or doubtful matters], liberty; in all things, charity."

In the essentials, stay unified. Remember that your class is not designed to serve as a subcommittee meeting or a de facto business meeting to discuss or decide these issues. You should always stand for essential doctrines in the appropriate venues. Do not entertain heavy discussion about how your or class members' beliefs or preferences differ from the pastor, staff, or church body. Paul reminded Timothy: "[Do not] give heed to fables and endless genealogies, which cause disputes rather than godly edification which is in faith. Now the purpose of the commandment is love from a pure heart, from a good conscience, and from sincere faith, from which some, having strayed, have turned aside to idle talk" (1 Tim. 1:4–6). Idle talk is translated as "fruitless discussion" in the Holman Christian Standard Bible. Emphasizing the differences in a public venue such as a Sunday school class will damage either your credibility or that of the person or group that you disagree with. Keep the focus on what you do agree on and if the disagreement is too severe, address it in the appropriate place rather than in your Sunday school class.

Ignoring or Being Inflexible About Curriculum

You may believe that you would be a better teacher if you had a better curriculum to work with. The reality is that good curriculum is not the key to making the teaching good. It is good teaching that makes the curriculum good. All curricula are not created equally. Some resources are definitely better than others. Get your hands on the best curriculum that you can to assist you in the preparation and presentation of your Bible study. However, once the decision is made by the leaders of the church, you should do the best you can with what you are given. Remember that the Scripture is ultimately the curriculum, and all other items are resources to assist you in teaching God's Word. Do not ignore the curriculum if it has been assigned and provided to you by the church leaders. Should you choose to ignore it, you will be sending a message to your members that you do not trust your leaders. Integrate the materials to the best of your ability and utilize your skills to make it even better. Do not be inflexible about the curriculum. You should make adjustments any time the material does not work or make sense to you. Do not steamroll through something when you know that it will not meet the need. Set it aside briefly when and if needed but do not discard it as irrelevant if it is the conviction and the strategy of the church to utilize a particular line of curriculum.

Putting People "On the Spot"

You should always seek to involve and interact with your

class or group as you teach God's Word. As you do so, be mindful that each member's level of comfort in participating may vary. Invite the audience to participate in the discussion and activities while being sensitive to the desire of some to learn in a more passive or less verbal manner. Be careful when you call on people to read, to pray, or to make comments. I have met people who do not go to Bible study because they were called on to read or pray. You may argue that people should not be so sensitive. Keep in mind that Sunday school is an open Bible study. It can be joined or visited at any point and is open to believers at all levels of maturity as well as non-believers. Invite and encourage people to participate without putting someone on the spot if you are unsure of their willingness to share without embarrassment.

Utilizing Closed Classes or Curriculum

You will find excellent curriculum to help Christians grow in their faith that may not be appropriate for a Sunday school class or open Bible study group. Some curriculum pieces require extensive preparation on the part of the participants and some require members to participate in every session from beginning to end in sequence. These resources are great as a supplement to Sunday school to take believers to a greater level of maturity. The same material can discourage members from inviting friends and disqualify guests from attendance if used in a Sunday school type of setting. Only use curriculum that requires minimal preparation for participants and encourages guests to attend Sunday school; offer the closed curriculum resources for smaller groups at other times to supplement the spiritual growth plan for your members.

Being a Unimethod Teacher

You can see that Jesus used lecture as a method when you read Matthew 5–7. Is that the only method He used? Certainly not! He used parables, word pictures, debate, question and answer, illustrations, field trips, drama, object lessons, visual aids, projects, and stories. The list here is just a sample of the methods Jesus used. Why did Jesus not solely rely on lecture? I believe you would agree that He was a master teacher. As our Creator He understood that humans possess a variety of differing learning styles. The combination of methods enhances the ability of all members of the audience to learn and understand what is being taught. Application cannot occur if there is not understanding. The fact that Jesus used so many methods should influence our teaching approach. Always use at least three or four different methods any time that you teach. Do not fall into the trap of being a unimethod teacher.

Disconnecting with the Maturity Level of the Audience

Do you teach preschool, children, students, or adults? The most effective way to teach adults is not the most effective way to teach children. Every age group has intellectual and sometimes physical nuances that affect the way you should communicate with them. You will also find some variations among adults that encompass an age span of up to eighty years. It is important that you discover the techniques that work best with the age group that you are assigned to lead. The inability to do so will result in a struggling ministry to the age group you serve, which may have a ripple effect on that group's parents or children. Seek to become an expert on methods for communicating to your audience. Do not dismiss this as an issue of the spirituality or maturity of your class rather than your responsibility to lead them effectively.

Neglecting Spiritual Dynamics

I have saved the most important point for last. Skills, techniques, and methods are of no value unless the Holy Spirit speaks to the hearts of the class or group members. Pray for your class. Pray for God's anointing on your teaching and for His Spirit to work powerfully through you as you communicate His Word. Grow in your skills so that you do not present any barriers to God working in the lives of those whom you are blessed to have in your group week after week as well as those who visit your class.

GETTING THOSE YOU LEAD TO APPLY WHAT YOU TEACH

James 1:22 says, "But be doers of the word, and not hearers only, deceiving yourselves." What good is a Bible study if people are not living what they are learning and if lives are not being changed? James says that we are *deceiving* ourselves if we think there is any value in *hearing* without *doing*. You need to lead your class to apply the message that you share to their lives during rest of the week. Consider the following four ideas for getting those you lead to apply what you teach.

Always spend time on personal application

Do not dismiss the Bible study without leading your class to discuss how the lesson of the day should affect their lives. Bible study is not a philosophical or an academic exercise. It is an encounter with God the Creator, Christ the risen Lord, and the Holy Spirit. You cannot be neutral or passive about a word from God. At the conclusion of the Bible study, ask participants to share a testimony of what God has said to them and how they should respond. You could also conclude by asking everyone to get in groups of three or four and take fifteen seconds each to share what they need to do in light of what they have learned. You will be reinforcing the necessity of application when you prompt these testimonies and discussions as well as when you share your personal experiences.

Review the previous lesson and share testimonies of application

Have you ever asked your class members, "Do you remember

what the lesson was last week?" That can be an awkward moment. I would suggest that you do not ask that question but that you do introduce each lesson with a two-minute review of the previous week. That will enable those who were absent to be brought up to date, refresh the memory of those who were present, reinforce what they learned, and open the door to consider how the lesson has been applied. You could also begin the Bible study by inviting someone to share an example of how last week's study affected his or her life during the week. I would encourage you to enlist someone in advance to attend the class or group who is prepared to share this testimony before you launch into the next Bible study. Your members will begin to understand that *doing* is as much an important part of the Sunday school experience as *hearing* what you have to share each week.

Regularly engage your class in missions and ministry opportunities

What is the last project that your class did together outside of the Sunday school hour? Remember that Jesus led the disciples to minister in the community. Work with your class or group to plan projects that you can do together in an effort to reach out to the lost and hurting. Your class cannot be "doers of the word" by isolating themselves inside a classroom for one hour each week. Remind your class that Jesus commands believers to "go."

Embrace the concept of releasing members to serve in other areas

The point has already been made but cannot be emphasized strongly enough. If you have the same number of people meeting week after week for months and years on end without ever going into the community together or releasing members to serve in other critical areas, you have missed the point! Do not forget that the preschool, children, and student ministries are counting on adult classes to raise up and send leaders to reach and teach boys and girls who will serve as the leaders of tomorrow.

Do you want to dig deeper in an effort to strengthen your preparation and presentation skills? Many excellent resources are available in your local Christian bookstore. I want to recommend five that I have found to be helpful. You may not like or agree with everything you read in these books, but they will all stretch you and help you to grow as a Bible teacher. Here they are:

> *The Craft of Christian Teaching* by Israel Galindo
> *The Seven Laws of the Learner* by Bruce Wilkinson
> *Teaching to Change Lives* by Howard Hendricks
> *Teaching with Style* by Bruce Wilkinson
> *Why Nobody Learns Much of Anything at Church and How to Fix It* by Thom and Joani Schultz

You will have to grow to be the teacher and leader that God wants you to be. It is a never-ending process. Your growth will not be complete until you go to be with the Lord. When and if you choose not to grow, you are inviting God to take you on home. Remember that you honor God when you grow and improve at what you do in order to accomplish His purpose for your life. A Sunday school that really works has a pastor and leaders who understand that sharpening the skills of the leaders continually is essential if the congregation wants to be positioned for God to bless them to see that the lost are reached, lives are changed, and leaders are sent.

DISCUSSION QUESTIONS

1. What is the training plan for your Sunday school leaders? What are the strengths and weaknesses? How can it be improved?

2. What are some ways that you can encourage and enhance the participation of your Sunday school leaders in training?

3. What are some key skills that need to be learned and applied by your Sunday school leaders?

SOME CLOSING THOUGHTS

But this I say: He who sows sparingly will also reap sparingly, and he who sows bountifully will also reap bountifully. (2 Cor. 9:6)

PERHAPS YOU ARE FAMILIAR WITH the ad campaign of the Staples office supply company. The marketing campaign urges the potential customer to imagine what life would be like if he or she possessed an "easy button." Wouldn't it be great if you could push the button whenever you encountered a difficulty and could summarize your success with the exclamation "That was easy!" I would be the first person in line to purchase such an item if it existed. I would also be delighted if I could purchase an easy button for you and your ministry. You and I are well aware that no such device will ever be available in our ministries.

I developed the theme of "Sunday School That Really Works" in order to communicate an important principle. A Sunday school that works requires a lot of work! It is a high-investment strategy that provides a high return when implemented correctly. The most unlikely response that you will hear from a leader that invests time and energy into the Sunday school ministry will be, "That was easy." Instead, the most likely response will be, "That was worth the effort." A pastor cannot take a passive, hands-off approach to Sunday school and expect it to work. A Sunday school teacher cannot invest a minimum amount of time and energy into his or her class and expect to bear fruit. Paul reminded the Corinthians that they could not make small investments and expect large returns (2 Cor. 9:6).

You reap a harvest in proportion to the amount of seed that is sown. Leading the Sunday school and teaching a Sunday school class is work. Leading the Sunday school is not easy, but it is a worthy investment of time and energy. Pastors and Sunday school teachers need to work arm in arm to pray, encourage, and motivate one another as they seek to apply the principles that enable the Sunday school to work to its fullest potential.

The work of the Sunday school is never complete. I cannot provide you with an activity, an individual principle, an idea, or a magic bullet that will propel your Sunday school toward months and years of effectiveness. You will have to continually work on applying a series of principles, and the work is unending. You will have to "sow bountifully" in order to "reap bountifully." You will find that it is worth the effort because the lost will be reached, lives will be changed, and leaders will be sent. Thank you for your willingness to make the investment.

I want to conclude by sharing five truths about a Sunday school that really works.

A Sunday school that really works is a strategy, not a program. It is a strategy that enables the church to engage the members in responding to the Great Commission. Sunday school is a strategy that provides an avenue to minister to all of the members, to provide Bible study that is age appropriate, to engage the congregation in evangelism, and to connect people to meaningful relationships. Sunday school really works when it is elevated as an essential strategy of the church that is intended to engage all members rather than an optional program where the highly committed gather for Bible study and fellowship.

A Sunday school that really works is a viable strategy. After hearing that his obituary had been published, Mark Twain replied, "The reports of my death are greatly exaggerated." Those who have declared the death of the Sunday school have exaggerated their claim that Sunday school is no longer a viable strategy. Congregations that have a good understanding and commitment to Sunday school growth principles are still flourishing in spite of what you may read on the Internet or hear from a church growth pundit. Purposefully engaging the congregation in a strategy to maximize participation in fulfilling the Great Commission will always bear fruit whether you call it the Sunday school or by any other name.

A Sunday school that really works is elevated and prioritized. You cannot devalue Sunday school as a strategy on the one hand and expect it to flourish on the other. The congregation will gravitate to that which the pastor elevates. The same is true for a denomination, a seminary, an association of churches, or for a Christian organization. A pastor and a congregation will naturally set priorities for the church. Sunday school will have to be included with the top priorities in order to work effectively.

A Sunday school that really works must have a Great Commission focus. The most common understanding of the purpose of Sunday school is that it is a Bible study. You are not incorrect in thinking of Sunday school in that manner, but you are incomplete in your understanding. The focus has been lost if the Bible study does not result in the lost being reached, lives being changed, and leaders being sent. A Sunday school that works has leaders who continually refocus the participants on the Great Commission.

A Sunday school that really works is a starting point. Keep in mind that Sunday school classes will not touch every life. The congregation must seek ways to minister to members of the community that may not ever respond to a Sunday school class. Sunday school classes will need to get into the community. Bible study groups and small groups need to be launched at other places and times in addition to Sunday morning prior to worship. A Sunday school that really works provides a foundation that maximizes participation by the congregation while affirming strategies that supplement and support the desire for the lost to be reached, lives to be changed, and leaders to be sent.

A Sunday school that really works is not easy. But, I have good news for you. Every Sunday school growth principle is within the reach of any volunteer or staff member willing to invest the time. I pray that you will find a way to obey the Great Commission and to express your love for Christ by engaging in ministries that are effective in the proclamation of the gospel message. I believe one of the ways that you can do so is by providing leadership for a Sunday school that really works.

Class Pretest

CONDUCT AN INFORMAL SURVEY OF your class using the following questions. Conduct the survey every six months to measure progress. Have each member of the class complete the following:

Please answer the following questions as honestly as you can. Your answers are confidential, and you do *not* need to include your name.

1. I have shared my faith with someone in the past three months.   Yes   No

2. I have participated in an organized activity/project/ mission with a group from our church in the past four months that was designed to share the gospel with people in our community.   Yes   No

3. The newest believer in our class is _____. He or she trusted Christ within the past twelve months.   Yes   No

   a. I attend worship on a regular basis.   Yes   No

   b. I attend our class/small group on a regular basis.
                                                      Yes   No

c. I have a personal devotional time most every day.

Yes No

4. I personally participated in a missions or ministry project in the past year.   Yes No

5. A leader from our church has interacted with me about my personal spiritual development in the past twelve months.   Yes No

6. I have a specific leadership responsibility in this class or group.   Yes No

7. My responsibility is _____

_____.

8. I have been equipped to share my faith.   Yes No

9. Members of our class/group are encouraged and affirmed when they leave to serve in other areas of ministry.   Yes No

10. My greatest spiritual need is: _____

_____.

APPENDIX B

Spiritual Growth Interviews

THE FOLLOWING ARE SAMPLE QUESTIONS to ask of class members in personal interviews. The purpose of the interviews is to determine spiritual growth, to assess needs, and to measure progress. You do not need to ask every question, and you do not have to write down the responses as you are asking the questions. You do need to take some time to write down responses soon after the interviews while the answers are fresh on your mind. Begin by asking informal questions about interest, hobbies, hometown, etc.

1. How long have you attended _____ church?

2. How did you come to know that you needed Christ as your Savior?

3. Where and when did you trust Jesus Christ as your Savior?

4. What are some of your greatest challenges as a Christian?

5. What are your spiritual gifts, passions, and talents?

6. What do you need from our Sunday school class to help you in your spiritual growth?

7. What needs to happen for our class to be more effective in helping the members to grow in their faith?

8. What needs to happen for our class to have a greater impact on our community?

9. What has God been doing in your life in recent weeks?

10. How may I pray for you in the coming weeks?

Sample Teacher Expectations in a Great Commission Sunday School

1. To prepare each week to lead a meaningful, age-appropriate Bible study for Sunday morning (2 Tim. 2:15).

2. To arrive and be in the classroom at least ten minutes early each Sunday to greet members and guests (James 2:1–9).

3. To maintain records to strengthen the group's pursuit of the overall purpose and mission of the Sunday school (Luke 15:1–7).

4. To organize the class for ministry to members and outreach to prospects (Exod. 18).

5. To participate in training opportunities as provided throughout the year (2 Tim. 1:6).

6. To enlist an apprentice teacher. To develop and send out leaders from your class to serve in ministry and to assist in creating new classes (2 Tim 2:2).

7. To set a positive example for others by living as an authentic witness of Christ and being fully involved in the life of the church (James 3:1).

Sunday School Guidelines for When You Must Be Absent

1. Do not announce your absence to your class in advance.

2. Do take responsibility for enlisting a replacement when you must be absent.

3. Avoid combining classes when possible (and do so only with the affirmation of the staff and/or Sunday school director).

4. Enlist an emergency substitute. Have them prepare a lesson for your class that can be taught on any Sunday and that can be taught with very short notice. Call this person as soon as you know you will be absent.

5. Contact staff and/or Sunday school director as soon as you know you will be absent.

6. It is understood that everyone will have to be absent on occasion but that frequent absences should be avoided.

BIBLIOGRAPHY

Crites, Tom. "Sunday School/Open Group Ministry: A Look at Statistics Related to Sunday School." Atlanta: GBC Research, 2004.

Francis, David. "Simple Churches Have Intentional Sunday Schools." *Facts and Trends*, November/December 2006.

Galindo, Israel. *The Craft of Christian Teaching.* Valley Forge, PA: Judson Press, 1998.

Hemphill, Ken. *The Bonsai Theory of Church Growth.* Nashville: Broadman & Holman, 1991.

_____. *Revitalizing the Sunday Morning Dinosaur.* Nashville: Broadman & Holman, 1996.

Hendricks, Howard. *Teaching to Change Lives: Seven Proven Ways to Make Your Teaching Come Alive.* Colorado Springs: Multnomah, 2003.

Hunt, Josh. *Your Class Can Double in Two Years or Less.* Loveland, CO: Group, 1997.

Jones, Laurie Beth. *Jesus: CEO.* New York: Hyperion Publishers, 2009.

Kelley, Charles S., Jr. *How Did They Do It? The Story of Southern Baptist Evangelism.* Covington, LA: Insight Press, 1993.

Lovelace, Libby. "Encouragement for Evangelism: Lifeway Research Studies 19 Standout Churches." *Facts and Trends*, May/June 2007.

Mims, Gene. *Kingdom Principles for Church Growth.* Nashville: Lifeway, 1994.

Parr, Steve. "Georgia's Fastest Growing Sunday Schools: Ten Common Factors." Atlanta: GBC Research, 2001. (Available in pdf format via "Resources" link at http://

www.gabaptist.org; locate under "Free Resources – SS/ Open Group.")

_____. *Georgia's Top Evangelistic Churches: Ten Lessons from the Most Effective Churches.* Atlanta: GBC Research, 2008. (Available via the online store at www.gabaptist.org.)

Patzia, Arthur G. *Ephesians.* In vol. 10 of The New International Biblical Commentary, ed. W. Ward Gasque. Peabody, MA: Hendrickson, 1990.

Rainer, Thom S. *Effective Evangelistic Churches.* Nashville: Broadman & Holman, 1996.

_____. *High Expectations.* Nashville: Broadman & Holman, 1999.

_____. *Surprising Insights from the Unchurched.* Grand Rapids: Zondervan, 2008.

Schultz, Thom, and Joani Schultz. *Why Nobody Learns Much of Anything at Church: and How to Fix It.* Rev. ed. Loveland, CO: Group, 1996.

Stein, Robert H. *The New American Commentary: Luke.* Nashville, Broadman & Holman, 1992.

Stetzer, Ed, and Mike Dodson. *Comeback Churches: How 300 Churches Turned Around and Yours Can Too.* Nashville: Broadman & Holman, 2007.

Taylor, Allan. *The Six Core Values of Sunday School.* Canton, GA: Riverstone, 2003.

_____. *Sunday School in HD: Sharpening the Focus on What Makes Your Church Healthy.* Nashville, Broadman & Holman, 2009.

Warren, Rick. *The Purpose Driven Church.* Grand Rapids: Zondervan, 1995.

Wilkinson, Bruce. *Teaching with Style.* Atlanta: Walk Through the Bible Ministries, 1994.

_____. *The Seven Laws of the Learner.* Colorodo Springs: Multnomah, 2005.